PROGRESSIVE

PIANO

for ADULTS

DESIGNED FOR THE ADULT BEGINNER

BY PETER GELLING

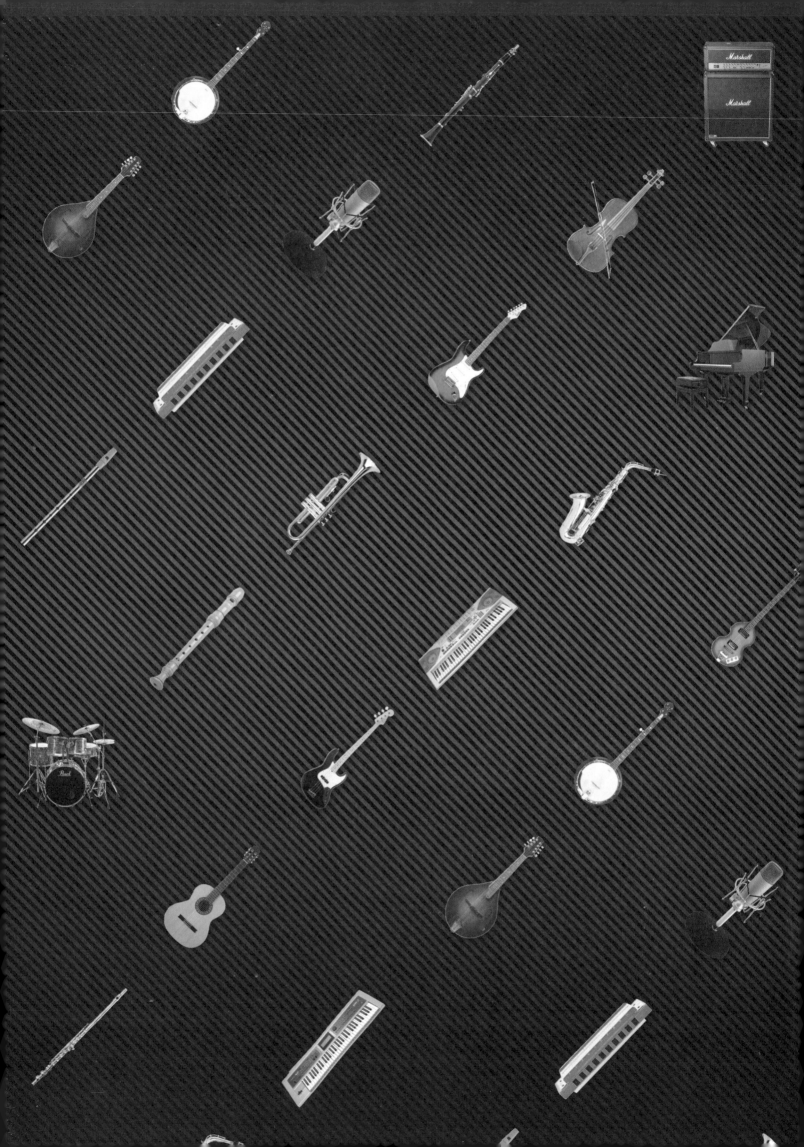

PROGRESSIVE PIANO FOR ADULTS
I.S.B.N. 978-982-9118-09-7
Order Code: 11809

For more information on
this series contact:
L.T.P. Publishing Pty Ltd
email: info@learntoplaymusic.com
or visit our website:
www.learntoplaymusic.com

Published by
KOALA MUSIC PUBLICATIONS ™

Contents

Contents Continued

Contents Continued

Introduction

Progressive Piano for Adults assumes you have no prior knowledge of music or playing pianos. In the course of the book you will learn all the essential techniques for both piano and electronic keyboard playing, as well as how to read music and understand music theory as it applies to piano playing. You will also learn many well known pieces and songs and get a great introduction to many styles of music, including Rock, Blues, Jazz, Folk and Classical.

The book begins by covering the basics of music reading and piano technique, concentrating on note memory, melody and accompaniment playing. Later lessons involve learning to move around on the piano and introduce a variety of new styles and techniques aimed at preparing you for group playing as well as giving you the skills to play many more advanced solo pieces.

All piano players should know all of the information contained in this book. By the end of the book, you will be well on the way to becoming an excellent piano player and will have many great sounding solo pieces under your belt as well as being ready to play in a band.

Approach to Practice

From the beginning you should set yourself a goal. Many people learn piano because of a desire to play like their favourite artist (e.g. Elton John), or to play a certain style of music (e.g. Rock, Blues etc.). Motivations such as these will help you to persevere through the more difficult sections of work. As your playing develops it will be important to adjust and update your goals.

It is important to have a correct approach to practice. You will benefit more from several short practices (e.g. 15-30 minutes per day) than one or two long sessions per week. This is especially so in the early stages, because of the basic nature of the material being studied. In a practice session, you should divide your time evenly between the study of new material and the revision of past work. It is a common mistake for semi-advanced students to practice only the pieces they can already play well. Although this is more enjoyable, it is not a very satisfactory method of practice. You should also try to correct mistakes and experiment with new ideas.

Using the Accompanying DVDs, DVD-ROM and CD

The accompanying discs contain video and audio recordings of the examples in this book. An exercise number and a play icon on a colored strip indicates a recorded example:

 57 ◄─── CD TRACK / DVD MENU NUMBER

The book shows you where to put your fingers and what techniques to use, and the recordings let you hear and see how each example should sound and look when performed correctly.

DVD View

Practice the examples slowly at first on your own. Then try playing to a metronome set to a slow tempo, such that you can play the example evenly and without stopping. Gradually increase the tempo as you become more confident and then you can try playing along with the recording.

You will hear a drum beat at the beginning of each example, to lead you into the example and to help you keep time.

Included with this book:

* **2 DVDs**, which can be played in any DVD player and contain video of all the exercises in this book and a full scrolling score (displayed above). You can choose between several audio options including 'main part with backing track' (so you can hear how the piano should sound with a band), 'solo main part' (so you can hear the piano by itself) or 'backing track only' (so you can play along). These audio angles (or language tracks) are accessed from the DVD remote.

* **1 DVD-ROM**, which can be used in any computer and most gaming consoles and portable media players (e.g. iPod, Xbox, Playstation etc) and contains all the audio and video for all exercises in this book. Both discs contain identical content but one is for use with Microsoft Windows Media Player (included free with all Windows PCs) and the other for Apple iTunes and Quicktime Media Player (included free with all Apple Mac computers and available for Windows PCs via free download at www.apple.com). On both discs you will find two folders, one containing the video examples and the other containing the audio examples. Follow the instructions for your media player to import these files to your hard drive and transfer to your portable media player if required.

* **1 CD**, which can be played in any CD player. Due to the limitations of the CD format not all examples are present on the CD.

Tips

* Most CD, DVD and portable media players have the ability to repeat tracks. You can make good use of this feature to practice the examples a number of times without stopping.

* The latest versions of both Windows Media Player and Quicktime Player (available with iTunes) have the ability to slow down the speed of the recorded exercises while still maintaining the correct pitch. This is very handy for practicing the more complex pieces.

How to Sit at the Piano

Sit up straight and relaxed. If your seat can move up or down, adjust it to a comfortable height. The instrument shown in photo 1 is an acoustic piano, but the sitting position is the same for all types of pianos.

Photo 1

Hand Shape

Always curve your fingers. This helps keep your fingers at the same level, as shown in photo 2.

Photo 2

When you play the keys on the piano, use the tips of your fingers, and the side of your thumb. See photo 3.

Photo 3

Music Notes

There are only **seven** letters used for notes in music. They are:

A B C D E F G

These notes are known as the **musical alphabet**. They are the names of the **white** keys on the piano.

Notes on The Piano

The black keys always appear in groups of two or three. The **C note** is a **white key**. It is always on the left hand side of a group of two black keys. Find all the C notes on your piano.

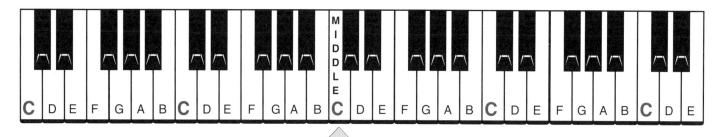

The first note you will learn to play is **Middle C**.
In this book, Middle C is indicated by a yellow triangle beneath the diagram.

How to Find Middle C

Middle C is the note in the middle of the piano. Play middle C with the thumb of your right hand, and then the thumb of your left hand.

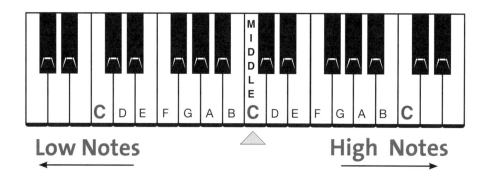

Low Notes ←   **High Notes** →

Fingers

Each finger has its own number.

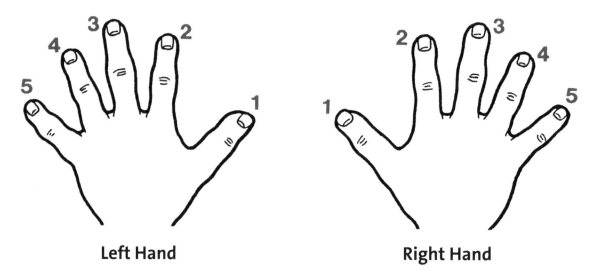

Left Hand   **Right Hand**

The **thumb** of each hand is counted as the **first** finger and has the number **1**.

How to Read Music

These five lines are called the **staff** or **stave**.
Music notes are written in the spaces and on the lines of the staff.

TREBLE CLEF

This symbol is called a **treble clef**.

BASS CLEF

This symbol is called a **bass clef**.

TREBLE STAFF

A staff with a treble clef written on it is
called a **treble staff**.

BASS STAFF

A staff with a bass clef written on it is called
a **bass staff**.

High notes are written on the **treble staff**, and are usually played with your **right hand**.
Low notes are written on the **bass staff**, and are usually played with your **left hand**.

The Grand Staff

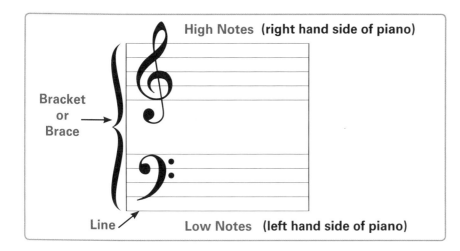

When the treble and bass staves are joined together by a line and a bracket, they are called a **grand staff**. Piano music is written on the grand staff.

Music is divided into **bars** (sometimes called **measures**) by **bar lines**. In this example there are **two** bars of music.

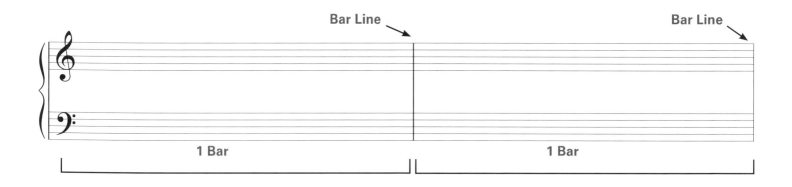

To remember the notes on the lines of the **treble** staff, say:

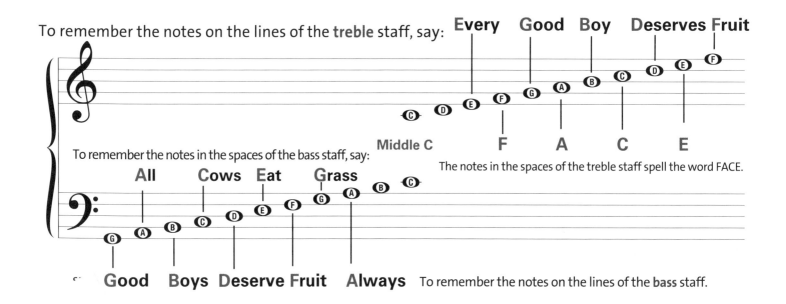

www.learntoplaymusic.com

Note and Rest Values

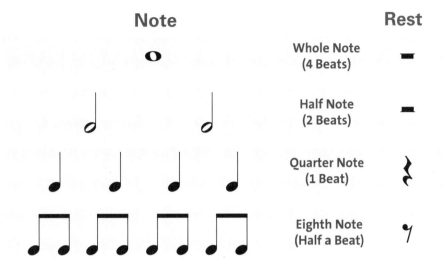

	Note	Rest
Whole Note (4 Beats)	𝅝	▬
Half Note (2 Beats)	𝅗𝅥	▬
Quarter Note (1 Beat)	♩	𝄽
Eighth Note (Half a Beat)	♫	𝄾

The Quarter Note

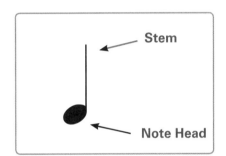

Stem

Note Head

This is a musical note called a **quarter** note. A quarter note lasts for **one** beat.

The Four Four Time Signature ($\frac{4}{4}$)

The two pairs of numbers after the clefs are called the **time signature**.

This is called the **four four** time signature. It tells you there are **four** beats in each bar. There are **four** quarter notes in a bar of $\frac{4}{4}$ time.

LESSON ONE

The Notes Middle C, D and E

Middle C is written just **below** the treble staff on a short line called a **leger** line. See page 10 to locate middle C on the piano.
• Middle **C** is played with the **first** finger (thumb) of your right hand.
• The **D** note is played with the **second** finger of your right hand.
• The **E** note is played with the **third** finger of your right hand.

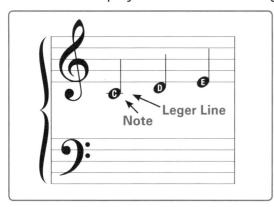
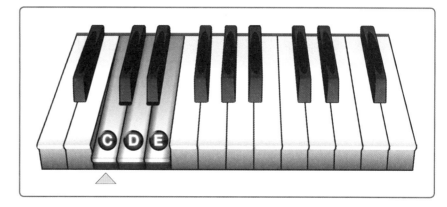

The Quarter Note

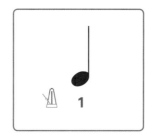

This is a **quarter** note. It lasts for **one** beat. There are **four** quarter notes in one bar of music in ⁴⁄₄ time.
The count is indicated below the notes, beginning with a metronome symbol (). A metronome is a time keeping device used by most musicians.

 **1.0**

In the following example there are **four** bars of music, **two** bars of **middle C**, **one** bar of the **D** note and **one** bar of the **E** note. There are four quarter notes in each bar.

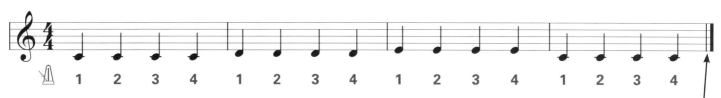

The **double bar** at the end indicates that the exercise has finished.

The Half Note

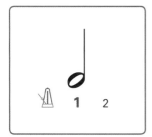

This is a **half** note. It lasts for **two** beats. There are **two** half notes in one bar of ⁴⁄₄ time.

The Whole Note

This is a **whole** note. It lasts for **four** beats. There is **one** whole note in one bar of ⁴⁄₄ time.

The **larger** bold numbers in the count indicate that a note is to be played. The **smaller** numbers indicate that a note is to be held until the next bold number (note).

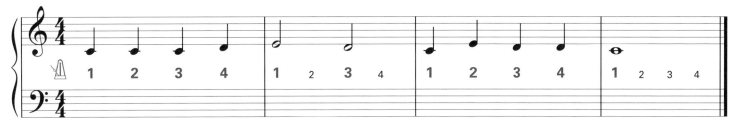

1.1 In the Light of the Moon

This song contains quarter, half and whole notes. Make sure you use the correct fingers and follow the count carefully.

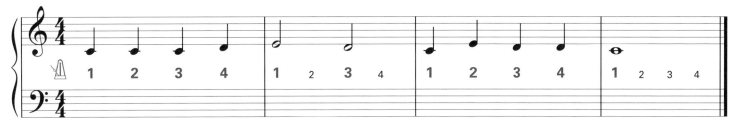

The Notes F and G

The note F is played with the fourth finger of your right hand.
The note G is played with the fifth finger of your right hand.

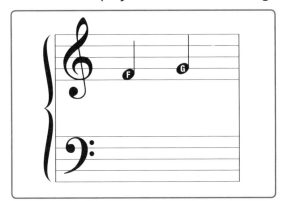

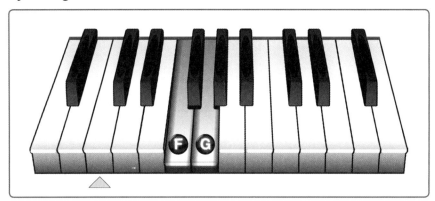

1.2 Aura Lee

The song **Aura Lee** contains 8 bars of music in $\frac{4}{4}$ time. Remember to count as you play to help you keep time.

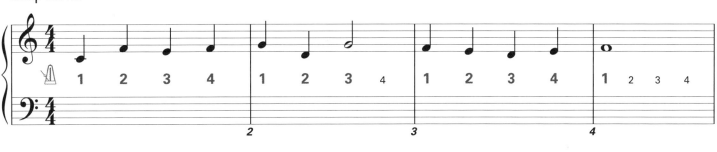

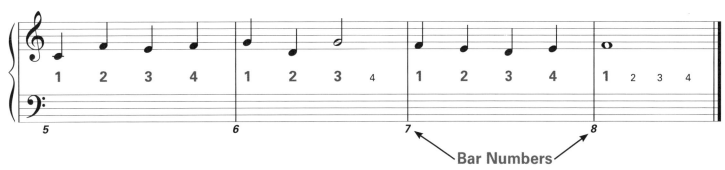

Bar Numbers

THINGS TO REMEMBER

1. Play the keys with the tips of your fingers. 2. Keep your fingers curved.

LESSON TWO

Chords

A **chord** is a group of notes which are played together. Chords are used to accompany the melody of a song. In the early stages, chords are usually played with the **left** hand and the melody is played with the right. The first chord you will learn is **C major**, usually just called the **C** chord.

The C Major Chord

The C chord contains three notes - **C**, **E** and **G**. To play the **C** chord use the **first**, **third** and **fifth** fingers of your left hand, as shown in the **C** chord diagram. In this book, the notes of major chords are shown in red.

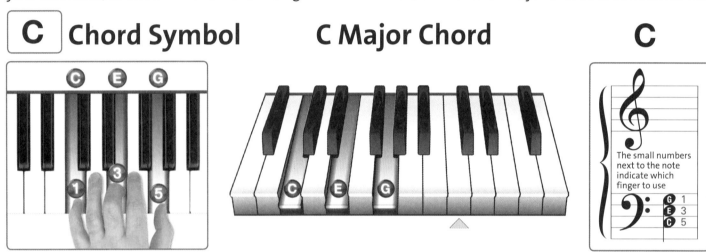

C Chord Symbol
C Major Chord
C

The small numbers next to the note indicate which finger to use

Seventh Chords

Another common type of chord is the **dominant seventh** chord, usually called a **seventh** chord. A **seventh** chord is indicated by the number **7** written after the chord name, eg: **G seventh** is written as **G7**.

The G Seventh Chord

The **G7** chord contains a new note - the **B** next to the C below Middle C. Play the B with the **fifth** finger of your left hand, and use your **first** and **second** fingers to play the G and F notes, as shown in the **G7** chord diagram. The notes in dominant 7th chords are shown in green.

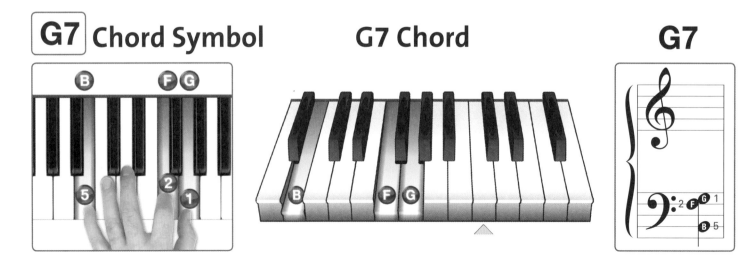

G7 Chord Symbol
G7 Chord
G7

Changing Chords

Practice changing between the **C** and **G7** chords. As both these chords contain the same **G** note, changing between them is quite easy because the **thumb** stays in the same position. It is important to always use the correct fingering when playing notes and chords.

The Whole Rest

This symbol is a whole rest. It indicates **four** beats of silence in $\frac{4}{4}$ time. **Small** counting numbers are placed under rests.

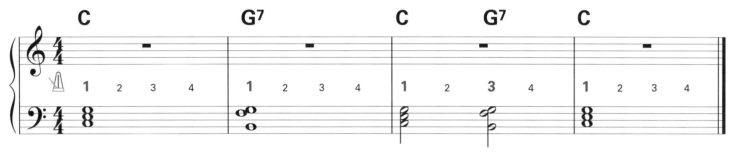

Chord symbols are placed above the staff. There are two chords in bar 3. Each chord receives **two** beats.

Songs With Chords

Before playing songs with chords, practice each part separately. First practice the **melody** of the song by itself (right hand part), then practice the **chords** by themselves (left hand part). Once you have learnt both parts, play them together. Practice slowly and evenly, and count as you play. The part containing the chords is called the **accompaniment**.

 2.1   Ode to Joy

This song is the main theme to **Beethoven's 9th Symphony**. It contains all the notes and chords you have learnt so far and has two chords in bar 8.

Ludwig van Beethoven

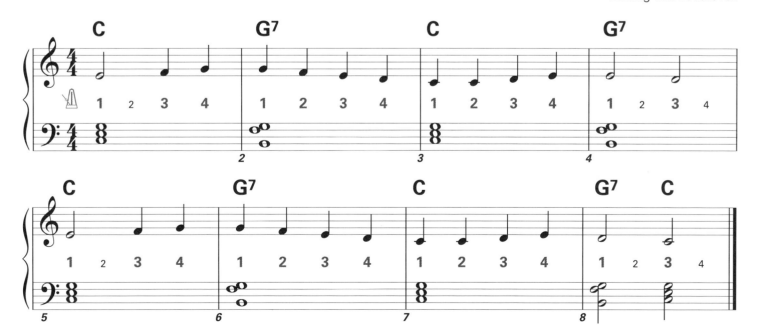

LESSON THREE

The Quarter Rest

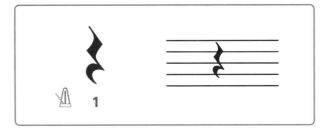

This symbol is a quarter rest. It indicates **one beat of silence**. Do not play any note. Remember that small counting numbers are placed under rests.

The Half Rest

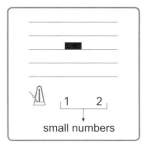

small numbers

This is a **half** rest. It indicates **2 beats** of silence.

3   Good Evening Friends

G⁷

One beat of silence

These two dots are a **repeat sign** and indicate that the piece is to be played again.

The F Chord

The next chord you will learn to play is the **F** chord. To play the **F** chord, use the **first, second** and **fifth** fingers of your left hand, as shown in the F chord diagram. The F chord introduces the note A below middle C.

F Chord Symbol   F Major Chord   F

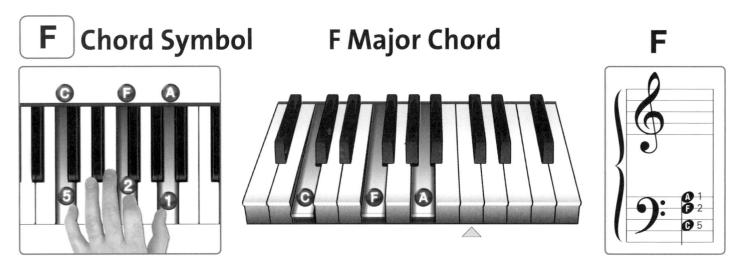

When changing between the **C** and **F** chords, keep your **fifth** finger in position as this note is common to both chords. When changing between the **F** and **G7** chords, keep your **second** finger in position as this note is common to both chords. Practice changing between **C, F** and **G7**.

The Lead-in

Sometimes a song does not begin on the first beat of a bar. Any notes which come before the first full bar are called **lead-in notes** (or **pick-up notes**). When lead-in notes are used, the last bar is also incomplete. The notes in the lead-in and the last bar add up to one full bar.

4   When the Saints Go Marchin' In

When the Saints Go Marchin' In is a Jazz standard made popular by brass bands in New Orleans. The song uses a lead-in and also contains both quarter and half rests. The **counting numbers** refer to the melody (right hand part). Instead of writing a chord symbol above each bar of music it is common to only to write a chord symbol when the chord changes, e.g. the first 6 bars of this song use a **C** chord.

LESSON FOUR

The Three Four Time Signature ($\frac{3}{4}$)

This time signature is called the **three four** time signature. It indicates that there are three beats in each bar. Three four time is also known as waltz time. There are three quarter notes in one bar of $\frac{3}{4}$ time.

The Dotted Half Note

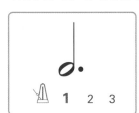

A dot written after a note extends its value by half.
A dot after a half note means that you hold it for **three** beats.
One dotted half note makes one bar of music in $\frac{3}{4}$ time.

5   Austrian Waltz

This song has dotted half notes in the left hand part. Once again, the counting numbers refer to the melody (right hand part). The left hand part is the **accompaniment** to the melody.

The Tie

A **tie** is a curved line that connects two notes with the **same** position on the staff. A tie tells you to play the **first note** only, and to hold it for the length of both notes.

6.0

Play the C note and chord and hold them for **six** beats.

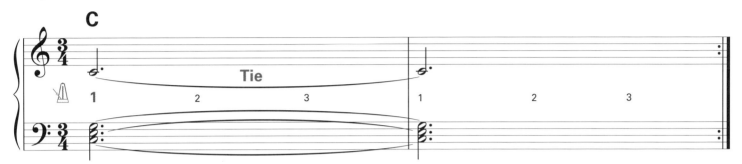

6.1   Marianne

This Caribbean folk song contains several ties which go across the bar line. Using ties is the only way of indicating that a note should be held across a bar line. Take care with the timing of the left hand part in this song.

LESSON FIVE

The Notes A, B and C

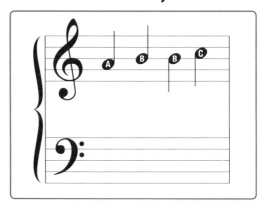 

Notes written above the middle line of a staff usually have their stems going down. Notes written below the middle line of the staff usually have their stems going up. The stem for the B note can go **up or down**.

The C Major Scale

A major scale is a group of eight notes that gives the familiar sound:

Do Re Mi Fa So La Ti Do

You now know enough notes to play the **C major** scale. To play the scale smoothly you will need to play the **F note** with your **thumb**. Do this by moving your thumb **underneath** your second and third fingers on the way up the scale. On the way down the scale, move your second and third fingers over your thumb. This is called the **crossover**. The small numbers placed above, below or beside notes on the staves tell you which finger to play each note with. Be sure to use the correct finger.

▶ 7

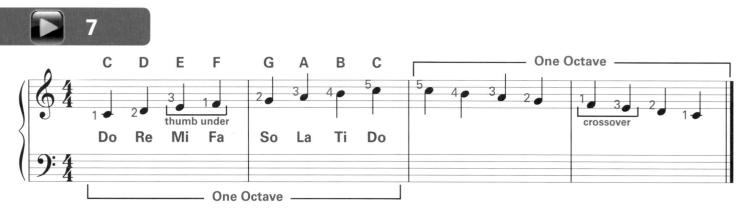

The Octave

An octave is the range of eight notes of a major scale. The **first** note and the **last** note of a major scale always have the **same** name. In the C major scale, the distance from Middle C to the C note above it (or below it) is one octave (eight notes). All the songs you have studied so far, and the next song, use notes from the C major scale. Pay close attention to any fingering numbers near the notes. It is important to use the indicated fingering, as this will make the songs easier to play. Use this same fingering every time you play the songs.

Here is an example using the descending C major scale. It ends with an octave leap from middle C to the C at the top of the scale.

The Eighth Note

This is an **eighth note**. It lasts for half a count. There are eight eighth notes in one bar of $\frac{4}{4}$ time

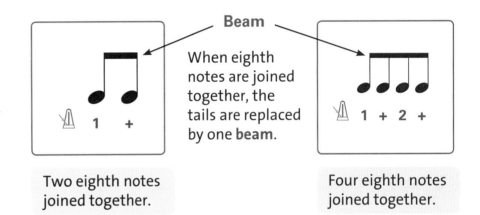

Beam

When eighth notes are joined together, the tails are replaced by one **beam**.

Two eighth notes joined together.

Four eighth notes joined together.

▶ 9.0   How to Count Eighth Notes

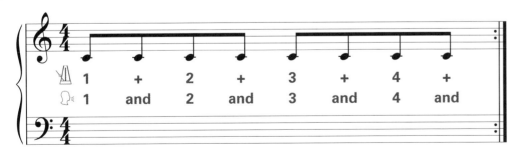

Staccato

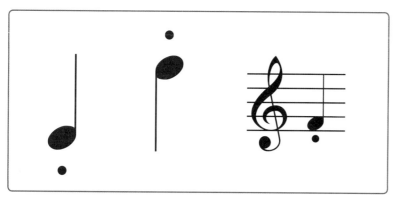

A **dot** placed above or below a note tells you to play it **staccato**. Staccato means to play a note short and separate from the other notes. To play a note short, lift your finger off the keys as quickly as possible.

 9.1 **Shave and a Haircut**

There are two eighth notes on the second beat of the first bar of this example. Play the notes and chords in the second bar staccato.

Key of C Major

When a song consists of notes from a particular scale, it is said to be written in the **key** which has the **same** name as that scale. For example, if a song contains notes from the **C major** scale, it is said to be in the **key of C major**. Nearly all the songs you have studied so far have been in the key of C major.

 9.2

LESSON SIX

The Bass Staff

Looking at the piano you can see that the same notes are repeated many times. So far you have learnt the notes **C D E F and G** on the treble staff, all played with the right hand. Notes played by the left hand are usually notated on the **bass staff**. Shown below are the notes C D E F and G on the bass staff. These notes sound exactly one **octave** lower than the same five notes in the treble staff.

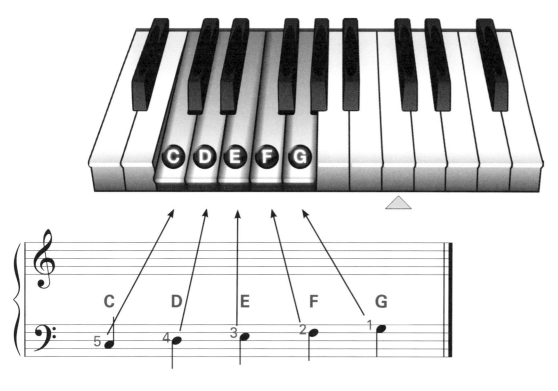

▶ **10.0   Aura Lee in the Bass Staff**

Here is the first part of the song Aura Lee written in the bass staff and then the treble staff.
Sing the names of the notes out loud as you play them.

Now play the following example which uses both hands together. Listen carefully and try to play the notes with both hands at the same time rather than being slightly separate or split.

▶ 10.1

Playing Chords with the Right Hand

It is also important to be able to play single notes with the left hand while playing **chords** with the right hand. The **G7** chord is played with the first, fourth and fifth fingers.

▶ 10.2

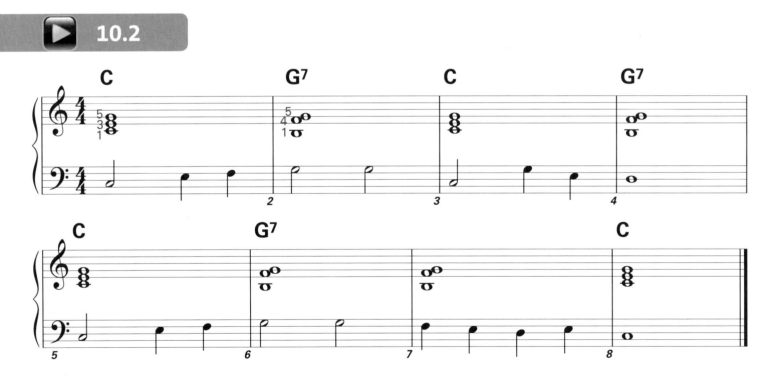

Playing Scales with Both Hands

The following example demonstrates the C major scale played with the left hand and then both hands together. The left hand fingering is the reverse of that of the right hand. The crossover occurs between **G** and **A**. When playing the scale with both hands together, the crossovers occur at different times with each hand, so take care not to lose your timing at these points. Play very slowly at first and only increase the speed once you can play the whole example smoothly and evenly.

11.0

11.1 Lavender's Blue (Melody in Bass)

In this English folk song, the melody is played with the left hand. Practice each hand separately if you need to.

LESSON SEVEN

Minor Chords

There are three main types of chords: **major**, **seventh** and **minor** chords. You have already learnt one major chord and one seventh chord. The first **minor** chord you will learn is the **D minor** chord. Minor chords are indicated by a small "**m**" written after the chord name, e.g. **Dm**. The notes in minor chords are shown in purple.

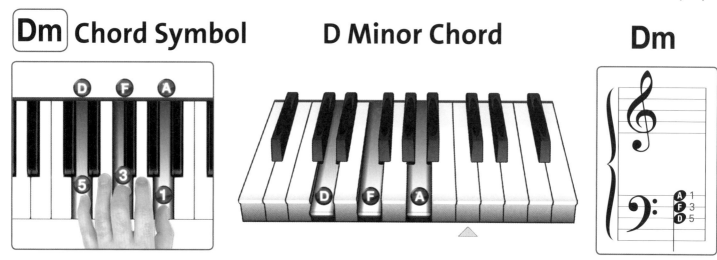

Dm Chord Symbol   D Minor Chord   **Dm**

To play the **D minor** chord, use the **first**, **third** and **fifth** fingers of your left hand. Once you are confident you know the chord, play it one octave higher with the right hand. As with the major chords, the fingering will be reversed for the right hand.

▶ 12.0

▶ 12.1

Next, practice changing between the chords **Dm** and **C**. Remember that the fingering is the same for both chords but the whole hand moves.

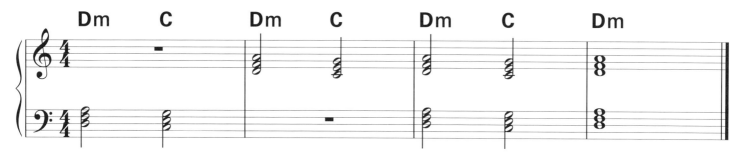

Five Finger Positions

In the following example, the right hand plays the melody while the left hand provides the accompaniment with the chords Dm and C. Notice the position of the right hand, with the thumb on the note D and the other fingers covering the notes E, F, G and A. This is often referred to as the D five finger position, or **D position** for short. Many of the previous examples have covered the notes C, D, E, F and G. This is known as the **C position**.

13.0

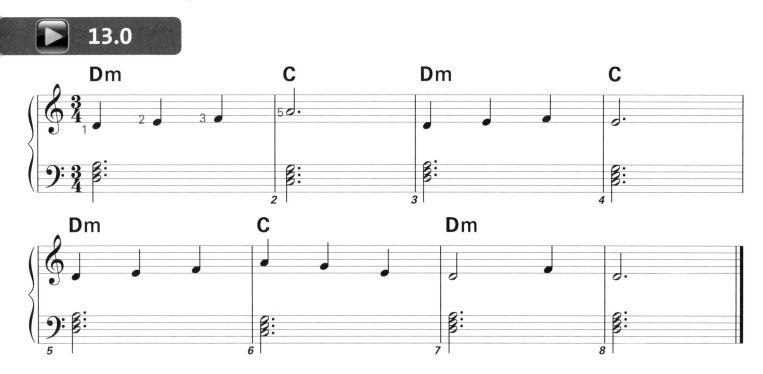

Piano Voices and "Timbre"

In the next piece both hands shift between the D position and the C position. On the recording, this example is played with an **organ** voice. This means the sound has a different tone quality (called "**timbre**") to that of a piano voice. Each instrument and human voice has its own particular timbre. Certain parts can sound great when played by one instrument, but terrible when the wrong one is used. Experiment with different instrumental voices on your piano when playing all the examples in the book.

13.1

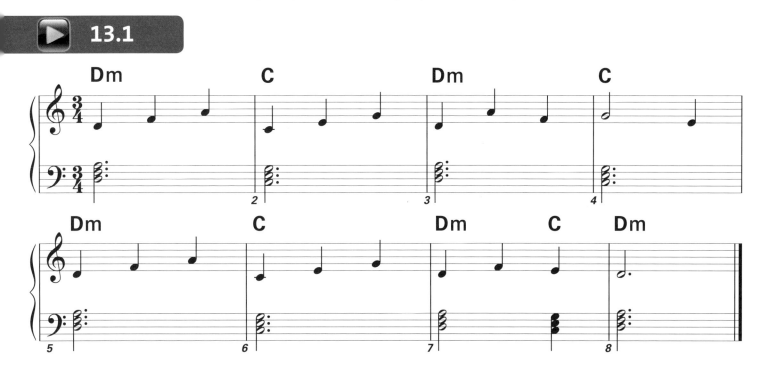

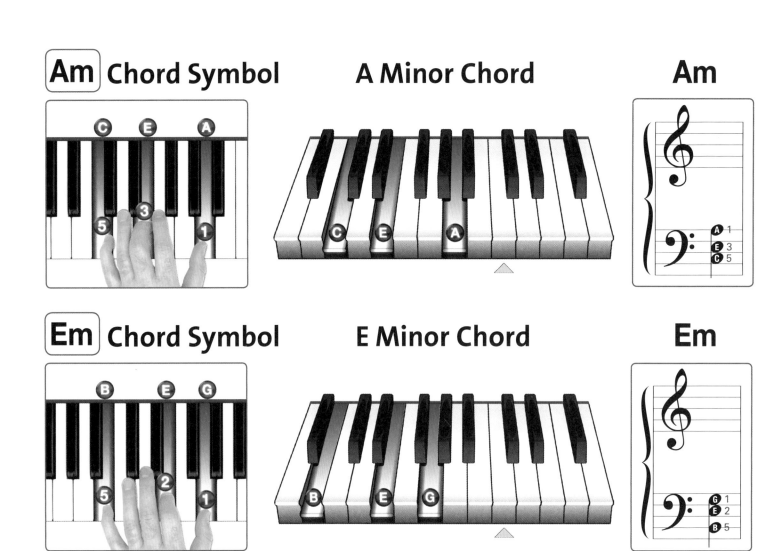

Am Chord Symbol — A Minor Chord — Am

Em Chord Symbol — E Minor Chord — Em

▶ 13.2

This example uses the chords **Am**, **Dm** and **Em**. The final bar contains two new low **A** notes, one played by each hand.

LESSON EIGHT

Arpeggios

An arpeggio is a chord played one note at a time. Arpeggios are often used by the left hand to accompany a melody played by the right hand. The following example demonstrates the chords **Dm** and **C** played as arpeggios.

14.0

The Dotted Quarter Note

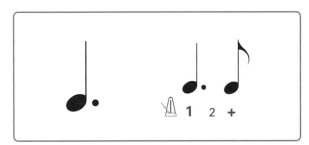

A dot written after a quarter note indicates that you should hold the note for **one and a half beats**. A dotted quarter note is often followed by an eighth note.

14.1

Scarborough Fair is a folk music standard. The accompaniment in this arrangement consists of arpeggios of the chords **Dm**, **C** and **F** played by the left hand. Take it slowly at first and practice each hand separately if you need to.

Broken Chords

Another common style of accompaniment is the use of broken chords. This style is similar to arpeggio playing except that the lowest note of the chord is the only one played by itself. The following example demonstrates broken chords in $\frac{4}{4}$ time.

15.0

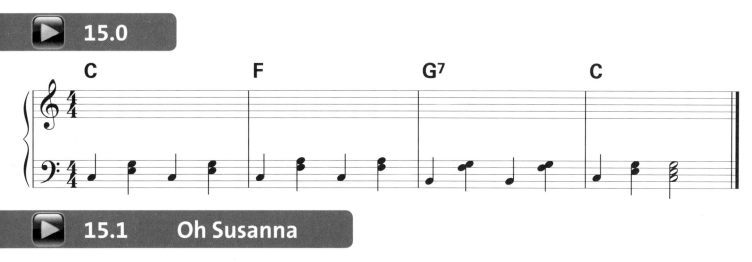

15.1 Oh Susanna

This traditional American folk song is played with a broken chord accompaniment. Once you can play it, try applying broken chord accompaniments to other songs you know.

LESSON NINE

Sharp Signs

This is a **sharp** sign.

When a sharp sign is placed before a note on the staff, it indicates that you play the key immediately to its **right**. This key may be either **black** or **white**.

The D7 Chord

The **D7** chord contains an **F sharp** note which is the black key immediately to the **right** of the F note (white key) below middle C. This **F♯** note is written on the **fourth** line of the bass staff. To play the **D7** chord, use the **first, third** and **fourth** fingers of your left hand as shown in the **D7** chord diagram.

D7 **Chord Symbol**   **D7 Chord**   **D7**

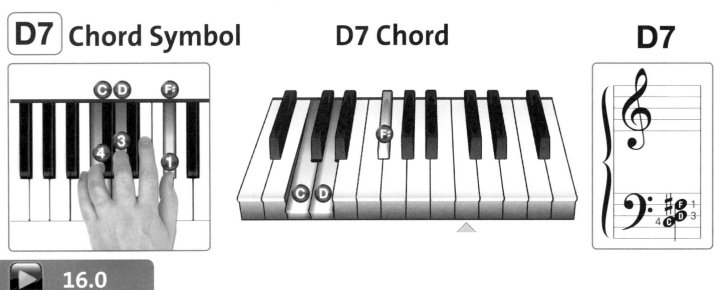

▶ 16.0

In this example, the **D7** chord is played by the left hand until the final bar, where it is played by the right hand. Practice changing between **D7** and **C** with both hands.

G Chord Symbol   G Major Chord   G

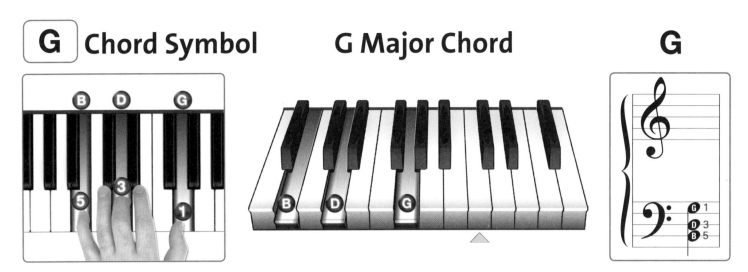

To play the **G** chord, use the **first**, **third** and **fifth** fingers of your left hand, as shown in the **G** chord diagram.

16.1   Hush Little Baby

The accompaniment to this popular children's song features **G** and **D7** played as broken chords.

Morning Has Broken uses all the chords you have learnt so far and is played with an arpeggio style accompaniment. If you have trouble co-ordinating both hands, practice each hand separately until you are confident playing each part and then combine them.

The Note F♯ (above Middle C)

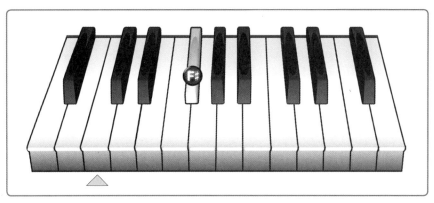

This **F♯** note is written in the **first space** of the treble staff.

This **F♯** note is the **black** key immediately to the **right** of the F note as shown in the diagram.

 18

This example makes frequent use of the note **F♯**.

Higher C Position

Continuing on with the concept of naming five finger hand positions from the lowest note, it is possible to quickly learn new notes. You have already learnt all the natural notes used in music: **A B C D E F** and **G**. As you know, all of these notes are repeated many times up and down the piano in different octaves.

Find the note **C** one octave above middle C with the first finger (thumb) of your right hand. Your remaining fingers will be covering the notes D, E, F and G. These notes are shown below on the treble staff.

 19   Ode to Joy (New Arrangement)

Here is the full melody of Ode to Joy using the notes from the new higher C position. Notice the alternating bass notes in the left hand part. This simple but effective form of accompaniment is used in many styles of music.

This piece summarises most of the things covered in the book up to this point. You now know eight chords and all of the different notes available on the white keys. Use what you have learnt to experiment and start creating some of your own music.

P. Gelling

Legato

The next song contains curved lines called **slurs.** A slur indicates that the notes written above or below it should be played **legato.** Legato means to play the notes smoothly, so that they sound connected to each other. Legato is the opposite of staccato. To play notes legato, keep your finger on the key until you have started to play the next key. This song also introduces a new high F♯ note one octave above the F♯ note you already know.

▶ 21.0   Sliding Down

▶ 21.1   Stepping and Sliding

This one contains the same notes as the previous example, but this time some of the notes are played staccato. When one hand is playing staccato it is easy to let the other hand follow.
However, none of the chords here are played staccato. Practice each part separately if necessary.

LESSON TEN

The G Major Scale

In Lesson 5, the C major scale was introduced. The **G major scale** starts and ends on the note **G**, and contains an **F♯** note instead of an F note. Play the following G major scale and notice that it still has the familiar sound **Do Re Mi Fa So La Ti Do**.

Key Signatures

The key of C major was discussed in Lesson 5. Songs that use notes from the **C major scale** are said to be in the **key of C major**. Similarly, songs that use notes from the **G major scale** are said to be in the **key of G major**. Songs in the key of G will usually contain **F♯** notes.

Instead of writing a sharp sign before every F note on the staff, it is easier to write just **one** sharp sign after each clef. This means that **all** the F notes on the staff are played as **F♯**, even though there is no sharp sign written before them. This is called a **key signature**.

This is the key signature for the key of **G major**. It has **one** sharp sign after each clef.

The C major scale contains no sharps or flats, therefore the key signature for the key of **C major** contains **no** sharps or flats.

This song is a traditional Irish dance tune, written here in the key of **G major**. Notice the key signature reminding you to play all F notes as **F♯**. The left hand accompaniment contains broken chords played **staccato**. Take care when changing from **G** to **D7** and practice the left hand by itself if you need to.

Practicing Scales

As mentioned previously, it is essential to be able to play both single notes and chords equally well with both hands. A good way of developing strength and independence in all the fingers is to practice scales with each hand and with both hands together. Shown below are various ways of playing the G major scale. First, here is the scale in the bass staff - to be played by the left hand. The first note is a new low G note. Notice the fingering written under the music - a crossover is necessary when moving between **D** and **E**.

 24.0   Left Hand

 24.1   Both Hands

Next, play the scale with both hands together. Play slowly and listen carefully. Don't rush! The most important thing is to play each note with both hands at exactly the same time, and to be sure all notes are even in length and volume. This time the right hand part begins with a new low G note. The crossovers occur at different times with each hand, so take care not to lose your timing at these points.

Once you can play a scale smoothly and evenly with both hands together, the next step is to play it over more than one octave. The following example shows the G major scale played in eighth notes over two octaves. The first note of the second octave is played with the thumb (1). This necessitates thumb under and crossover techniques. Take them slowly at first and only increase the speed once it is totally comfortable.

 24.2   Both Hands Over Two Octaves

The Common Time Signature

This symbol is called **common time**. It means exactly the same as $\frac{4}{4}$.

 25   **Changing Lanes**

This example in common time will put your scale practice to good use. The melody is played first by the left hand and then the right. The hands reverse roles every four bars.

P. Gelling

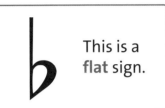

LESSON ELEVEN

Flat Signs

This is a **flat** sign.

When a **flat sign** is placed before a note on the staff, it means that you play the key immediately to its **left**. This key may be either black or white. The note **B flat** (written as **B♭**) is shown on the staff below in both treble and bass.

The Note B♭ (Treble and Bass)

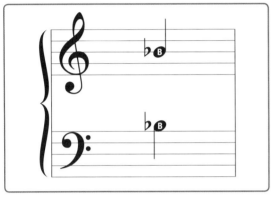

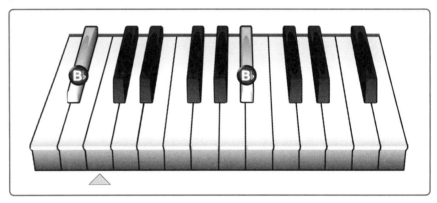

These **B♭** notes are written on the **third** line of the **treble staff** and above the top line of the **bass staff**.

The **B♭** note is the **black** key immediately to the left of the B note, as shown in the diagram.

▶ **26   Ghost of the Moor**

This piece uses both the **B♭** notes shown above. Playing single note lines with both hands is often more difficult than a melody accompanied by chords. Practice each hand separately if you need to.

P. Gelling

C7 Chord Symbol   C7 Chord   C7

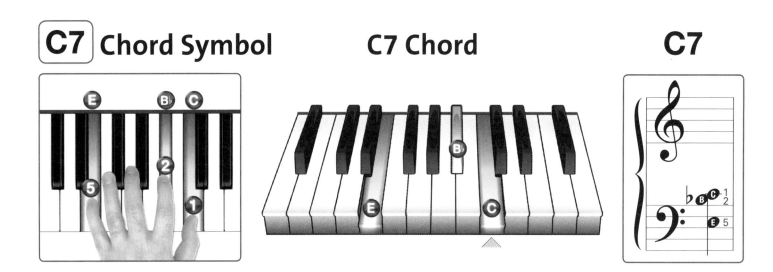

Key Signature of F Major

Instead of writing the flat sign before every B note on the staff, **one** flat sign can be written after each clef. This means that **all** B notes on the staff are played as **B♭**, even though there is no flat sign written before them. This is the key signature for the **key of F major**. There is **one** flat sign after each clef.

27

Practice changing between the chords **F** and **C7** with the left hand only before playing this example. Take it slowly and only increase the tempo when you can play it perfectly.

B♭ Chord Symbol B♭ Major Chord B♭

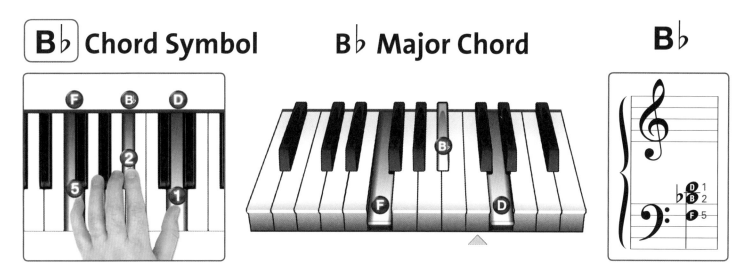

To play the **B♭** chord, use the first, second and fifth fingers of your left hand as shown in the B♭ chord diagram. Practice changing between **F** and **B♭** and also **B♭** and **C7**.

▶ 28 Shortnin' Bread

Notice the quick changes between **F** and **B♭** in this song. This style of accompaniment is common in Blues and Boogie piano playing. These styles will be dealt with later in the book.

The F Major Scale

The **F major scale** starts and ends on the note **F**, and it contains a **B♭** note instead of a B note. Play the F major scale below and listen for the **Do Re Mi Fa So La Ti Do** sound. Songs that use notes from the F major scale are in the **key of F major** and hence contain the note **B♭**. When playing the F major scale, take care with the fingering as the crossover point is different to that of the C and G major scales.

Here is the F major scale played over two octaves with both hands. It begins with two new **F** notes. To become familiar with the notes of the scale, name the notes out loud as you play. Memorize the fingering, take care with the crossover points in both hands, and practice each hand individually as well as both together. As always, clarity and evenness are more important than speed.

This song is in the key of **F major** and contains a variation on the broken chord style of accompaniment. As with previous examples, practice each hand separately if you need to.

P. Gelling

LESSON TWELVE
Using the Whole Piano

So far you have learnt notes from a low F to a high G covering a range of just over 3 octaves.
By learning the new notes shown on the staff and piano below you will be able to play over a range of
4 octaves, which covers most music.

▶ **31.0**

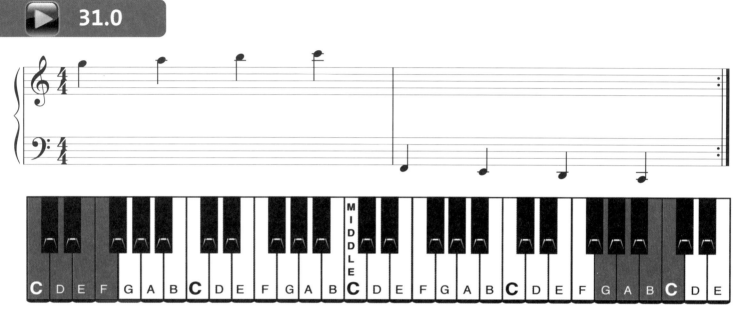

Now try playing a C major scale over four octaves. The low C shown here is the lowest note on some
pianos, but not on a piano or full length piano .

▶ **31.1**

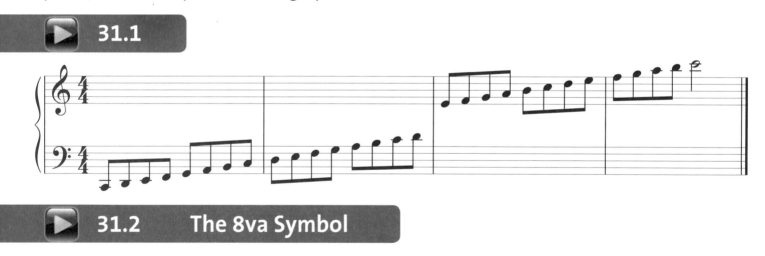

▶ **31.2   The 8va Symbol**

The following phrase has the symbol **8va** above the music. This means it is played an octave higher than
written. This symbol is often used for very high notes, as it makes them easier to read. When the notation
returns to its normal pitch, the word **loco** is written above the music.

Chord Inversions

So far you have learnt the C, F and G major chords. Because the lowest note in each of these three chords is the root note, the shape given is called the **root position**.

All major chords contain three different notes. These notes can be duplicated and/or played in a different shape. When the third (3) is the lowest note of the chord shape, the chord is said to be the **first inversion**. The diagram below illustrates the first inversion of the **C major** chord, which contains the notes **E** (3), **G** (5), and **C** (1) in that order.

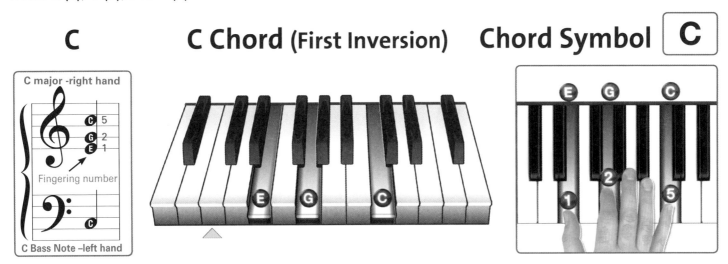

Do not confuse the fingering numbers on the chord diagrams with the interval numbers of the chord.

When the fifth (5) is the lowest note of the chord shape, the chord is said to be the **second inversion**. The diagram below illustrates the second inversion of the C major chord, which contains the notes **G** (5), **C** (1), and **E** (3) in that order.

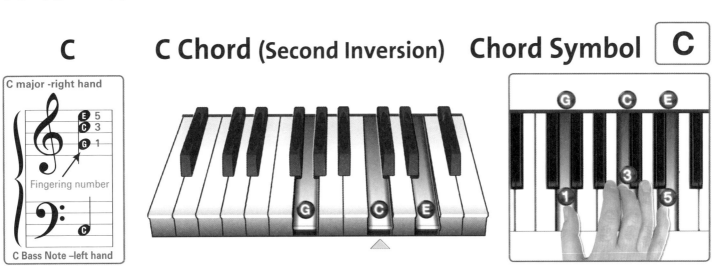

C Major Chord Inversions

The example below uses root position, first inversion, second inversion, and an octave of the root position of the C chord in the right hand part. Use the correct right hand fingering as shown on the notation accompanying the diagrams.

32.0

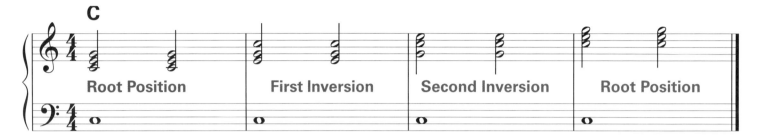

Root Position   First Inversion   Second Inversion   Root Position

G Major Chord Inversions

These three diagrams illustrate the root position (1 3 5), first inversion (3 5 1), and second inversion (5 1 3) of the G chord.

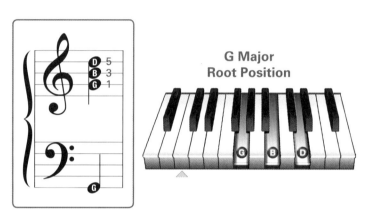

G Major Root Position

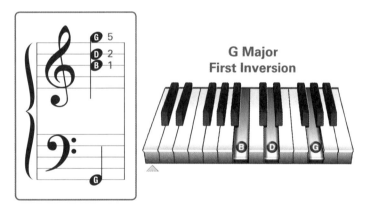

G Major First Inversion

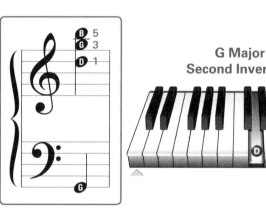

G Major Second Inversion

The following example uses the root position, first inversion, second inversion, and an octave of the root position of the **G** chord. Once again, remember to use the correct fingering as shown in the notation alongside the diagrams.

32.1

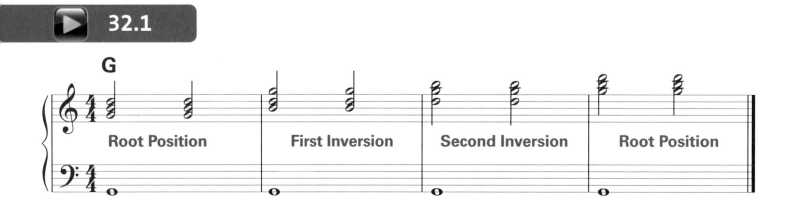

Root Position   First Inversion   Second Inversion   Root Position

F Major Chord Inversions

These three diagrams illustrate the root position (1 3 5), first inversion (3 5 1), and second inversion (5 1 3) of the F chord.

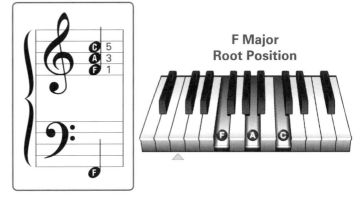

F Major
Root Position

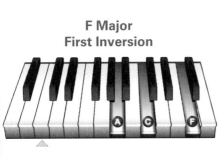

F Major
First Inversion

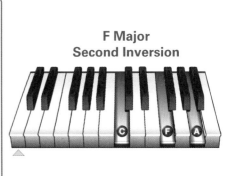

F Major
Second Inversion

 32.2

This example shows the root position, first inversion, second inversion, and an octave of the root position of the F chord.

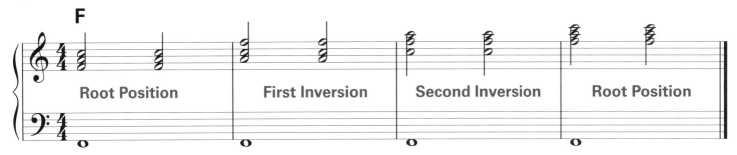

| Root Position | First Inversion | Second Inversion | Root Position |

 32.3

One of the reasons inversions are so useful is that they enable you to find chord shapes which are close together on the piano. Here the **C** chord appears in **root position**, the **F** chord is in **second inversion** and the **G** chord is in **first inversion**. The left hand plays the root note of each chord.

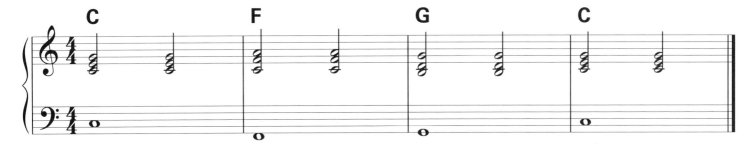

Here are some examples showing typical uses of these inversions. Notice how much easier the chord changes are. By using inversions which are close together, it leaves you free to concentrate on other important things such as rhythm.

33.0

33.1

33.2

Tempo Markings

The term **tempo** refers to the **speed** at which music is played. Tempo markings come from Italian words and some of them are listed below, along with their English translations. It is important to be able to recognize these markings and to be able to play comfortably at each tempo.

Adagio (slowly)   **Andante** (an easy walking pace)   **Moderato** (a moderate speed)

Allegro (fast)   **Presto** (very fast)

34   Waltzing Inversions

P. Gelling

The Eighth Rest

This symbol is an **eighth rest**. It indicates **half a beat** of silence.

Here is an example which makes use of eighth rests on the first and third beats in the right hand part. Be sure to keep your timing steady with the left hand and count as you play.

 35.0

Syncopation

In the following example all the eighth notes are played off the beat. Playing off the beat creates an effect known as **syncopation**, which means displacing the normal flow of accents (usually from on the beat to off the beat). Syncopated rhythms can be difficult at first but are common in many styles of music, so stick with it. Count and tap your foot to keep time as you play.

 35.1

Here are some more syncopated parts created by the use of eighth rests on the beat.

35.2

35.3

Doubling Notes in Chords

The chords in the next two examples contain four notes. Because there are only three different notes in a major chord, this means that some of the notes are **doubled**. The most commonly doubled notes are the **root** and the **fifth**. Playing four note voicings requires a greater stretch between the fingers, so be patient and practice the chords by themselves at first.

36.0

Here is a simple Country progression using four note chord voicings lower down on the piano. When you are accompanying other musicians, the pitch at which you choose to play largely depends on what the singer or other musicians are playing. Every instrument and voice has its most comfortable range or **register**. When playing with others, it is important not to clutter one register and leave too much space in others. As a piano player, you have more choice than singers or many other instrumentalists, so it is up to you to judge which register sounds best for your particular part.

Always think of what will serve the overall sound best.

LESSON FOURTEEN

Minor Chord Inversions

These three diagrams illustrate the root position (1 ♭3 5), first inversion (♭3 5 1), and second inversion (5 1 ♭3) of the **Am** chord.

Am Root Position

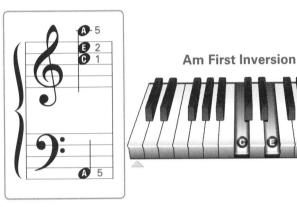

Am First Inversion

Am Second Inversion

The following example uses the root position, first inversion, second inversion, and an octave of the root position of the **Am** chord. Use the fingerings shown in the diagrams.

 37.0

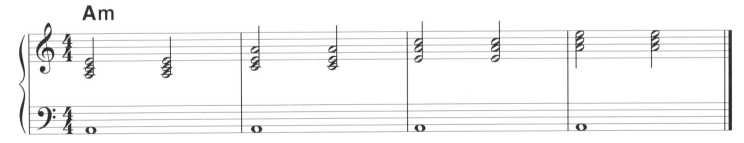

Here is a piano part making use of all three inversions of the A minor chord. Notice the interplay between the two hands in this part.

 37.1

Slash Chords

The following examples make use of another important piano technique: of playing a chord with the right hand over a specific bass note. Sometimes this note is different to the notes contained within the chord. In the example below, the symbol **G/E** occurs. This indicates a **G chord** played over an **E bass note**. This is called a **slash chord**. Slash chords can create many different harmonic effects. Each combination has a specific name and often creates an entirely new chord. This will be discussed later in the book. Basically you can play any chord over any bass note as long as it sounds good. Experiment with playing all the chords you have learnt over various bass notes from the C major scale.

In this example the chords are played as arpeggios.

Turnaround Progressions

A **turnaround** progression is a set pattern of chords that repeats itself. There are hundreds of well known songs based on turnaround progressions. All these songs contain basically the same chords in the same order. A turnaround may repeat over any number of bars. Usually 2, 4 and 8 bars. However, the **chord sequence** remains the same. Most Turnarounds contain at least one minor chord. The following turnarounds contain the chords **C**, **Am**, **F** and **G**.

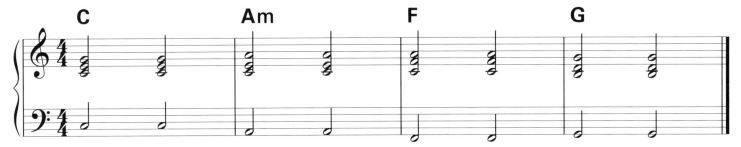

Accents

An important expressive technique on any instrument is the use of **Accents**. An accent marking tells you to play the note louder than other notes. There are two common types of accents which are shown below. The **long accent** is indicated by a **horizontal** wedge mark above or below the note. The **short accent** is indicated by a **vertical** wedge mark. Listen to the following example on the CD to hear the effect of accents.

Long accent   Short accent

Here are some more examples which use accents. They are all turnaround progressions played in different positions on the piano.

39.2

39.3

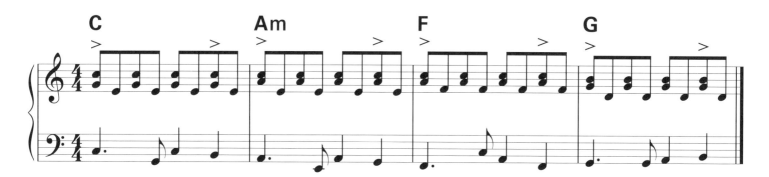

39.4

This one contains a repeated note pattern which results in a built–in accented rhythm. Experiment with this type of playing to create your own parts.

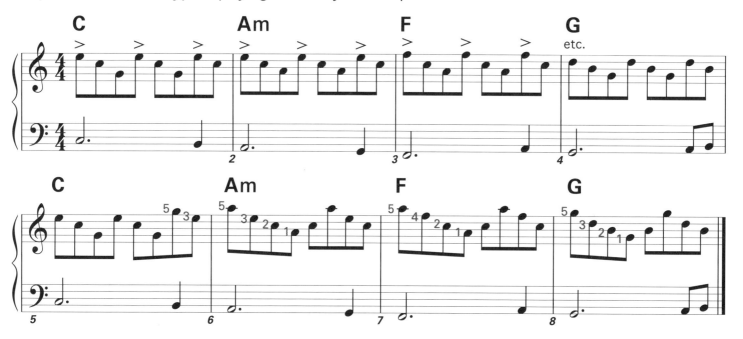

D Minor Chord Inversions

These three diagrams illustrate the root position (1 ♭3 5), first inversion (♭3 5 1), and second inversion (5 1 ♭3) of the **Dm** chord.

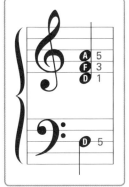
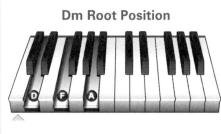

Dm Root Position

Dm First Inversion

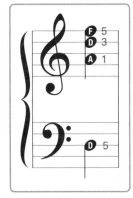
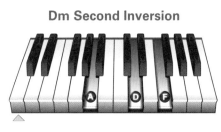

Dm Second Inversion

E Minor Chord Inversions

These three diagrams illustrate the root position (1 ♭3 5), first inversion (♭3 5 1), and second inversion (5 1 ♭3) of the **Em** chord.

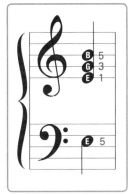
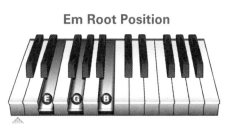

Em Root Position

Em First Inversion

Em Second Inversion

The following example uses all three inversions of the chords **D minor** and **E minor**.

 40.0

The following examples are common variations on the basic Turnaround progression. These examples all use the chords **Dm** and **Em**. Once you have them under your fingers, try playing the chords as arpeggios and experimenting with different inversions and different rhythms.

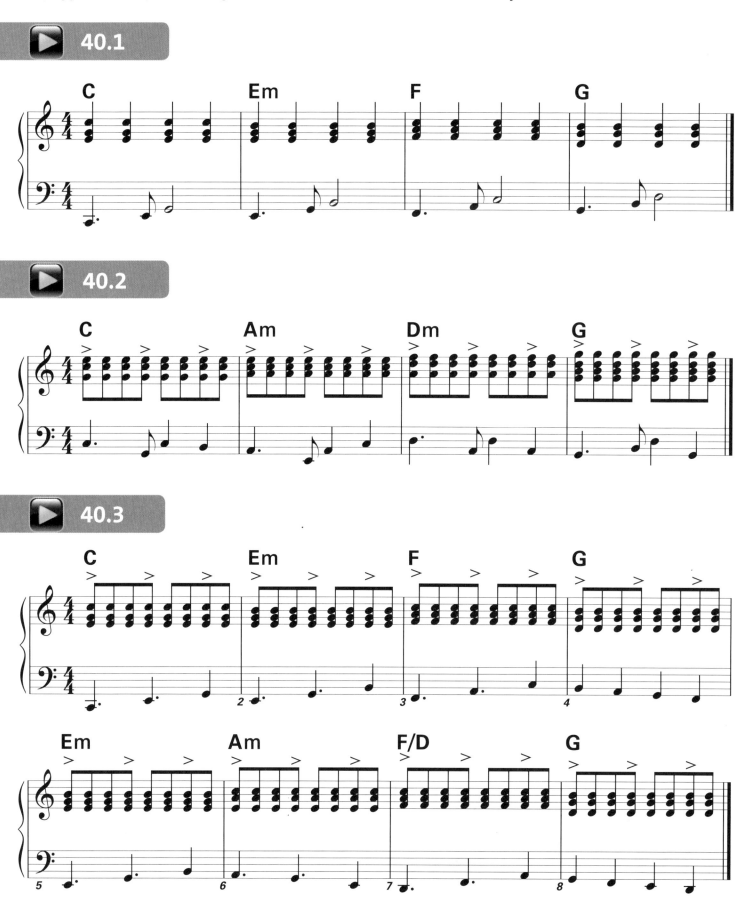

LESSON FIFTEEN

More About Syncopation

The use of **ties** is a common way of creating syncopated rhythms. The following example contains two bars of music using an Am chord. The first bar contains a rhythm of four eighth notes followed by a half note. In the second bar, the last eighth note is tied to the half note. Listen to the difference this makes to the rhythm. The use of ties in this manner is sometimes described as giving the rhythm a **push**.

▶ **41.0**

Experiment with groups of eighth notes and ties in various parts of the bar as shown in the following examples.

▶ **41.1**   **41.2**

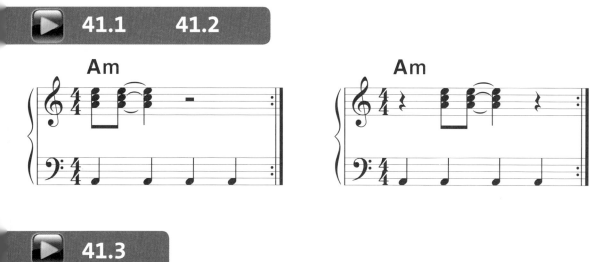

▶ **41.3**

Using a **push** is common between the last note of one bar and the first of the next bar.

Identifying Eighth Note Rhythms

There is a simple system for identifying any note's position in a bar by naming notes off the beat according to which beat they come directly after. The system works as follows: within a bar of continuous eighth notes in ⁴⁄₄ time, there are **eight** possible places where notes could occur. The first beat is called **one** (1), the next eighth note is called the "**and of one**", then comes beat **two**, the next eighth note is called the "**and of two**", then beat **three**, followed by the "**and of three**", then beat **four**, followed by the "**and of four**" which is the final eighth note in the bar. These positions are shown in the notation below.

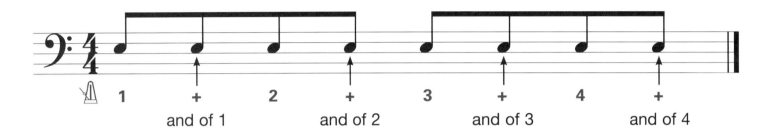

This system is particularly useful if you are having trouble with the timing of a rhythm. You simply identify where the notes occur in relation to each beat and then count them slowly until you have memorized the rhythm. Here is how the system can be used to analyze rhythms. In the right hand part of the following example, the chords are played on **2**, the **+ of 3** and the **+ of 4** in the first bar, and the last note in the bar is tied to a whole note which is held for the length of the second bar. The whole rhythm then repeats every two bars. Try analyzing the left hand part in this manner and write the count between the staves if necessary. Use this method every time you have trouble with a rhythm.

Pedal Tones

This example once again uses slash chords. This time, all three chords are played over the one bass note. When moving chords are used over a bass note, the bass note is described as a **pedal tone**, or **pedal note**. Pedal tones occur in many different styles of music and were extensively used by classical composers. This piece features a rhythm using dotted quarter notes and ties. It is called a **Charleston rhythm**, which is common in Rock, Jazz and Blues. Analyze it using the system shown on the previous page and count out loud as you play.

42.1

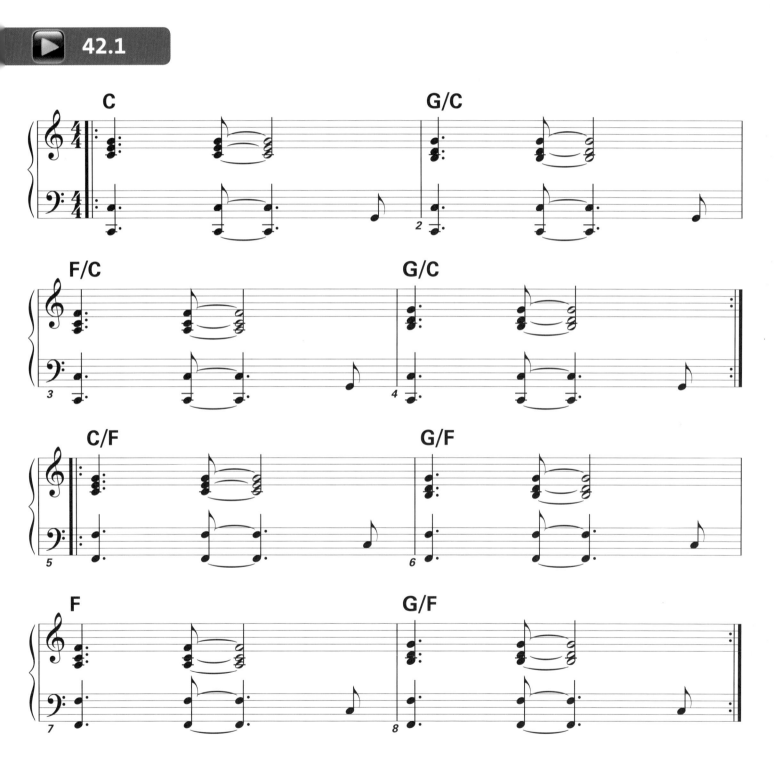

LESSON SIXTEEN

The Sixteenth Note

This is a **sixteenth note**.
It lasts for **one quarter** of a beat.
There are **four** sixteenth notes in
one beat. There are **16** sixteenth
notes in one bar of $\frac{4}{4}$ time.

Two sixteenth notes
joined together.

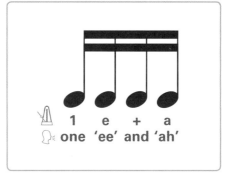

Four sixteenth notes joined together.

43.0   How to Count 16th Notes

When counting 16th notes, notice the different sound for each part of the beat –
one ee and ah, two ee and ah... etc (written **1 e + a, 2 e + a**... etc).

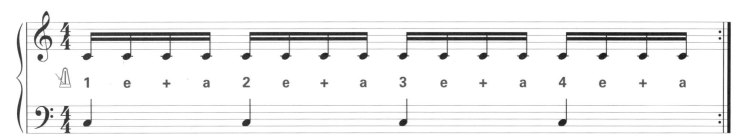

43.1

As with any new note value, it is important to practice your scales using 16th notes until you are
comfortable with them. Here is the **C major scale** played in sixteenth notes over four octaves.
Take it slowly at first, and remember to use your metronome and count out loud as you play.

This traditional American folk song features several 16th note passages. Although many of the eighth notes are played staccato, all the **16th notes** should be played **legato**. Practice each hand separately until you are comfortable with both parts and then put them together. If you have trouble co-ordinating the two hands, practice one bar at a time very slowly and only increase the speed when you can play the whole piece.

Allegro

Dynamics

The term **dynamics** refers to the **volume** at which music is played. If all music was played at the same volume it would lack expression and soon become boring. Therefore it is necessary to be able to play at a variety of dynamic levels ranging from very soft to very loud. There are various markings for dynamics in written music. Most come from Italian words. Some of these are listed below, along with their English translations. To practice dynamics, play a scale and then a melody at each of these volumes.

pp **pianissimo** (very soft)   *p* **piano** (soft)   *mp* **mezzo piano** (moderately soft)

mf **mezzo forte** (moderately loud)   *f* **forte** (loud)   *ff* **fortissimo** (very loud)

Volume Changes

crescendo   **diminuendo**

Gradual changes in volume are indicated by the **crescendo** (meaning a gradual increase in volume) and the **diminuendo** (meaning a gradual decrease in volume). Listen to the way they are applied to the scale in the following example.

▶ **45.0**

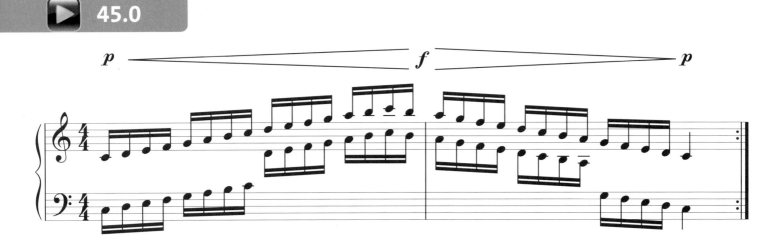

Learning to use dynamics effectively takes quite a while. A good way to practice dynamics is to play a basic rhythm (e.g. two bars of eighth notes) on one note but at different dynamic levels, ranging from as softly as you can play to as loudly as you can play. Then try the same thing with a short melody.
These two extremes are not so difficult, although keeping all the notes consistent when playing very quietly can be tricky at first. Most beginners have trouble making the grades of volume in between *pp* and *f* distinguishable, so be patient and keep practicing until you are comfortable with all the dynamic levels shown above.

Once you are comfortable with different dynamic levels, start adding crescendos and diminuendos. Again, start with one note until you are comfortable with gradual and consistent volume changes, then try crescendos and diminuendos with scales and finally with melodies. An instrumentalist with good control of dynamics and time will always be in demand with other musicians and well appreciated by audiences.

Here is a sixteenth note study by Classical composer **Carl Czerny**. It contains several dynamic markings including a crescendo over two bars. The way you use dynamics can make a huge difference to the feeling of the music and the response it evokes in a listener.

LESSON SEVENTEEN

Accidentals

Sometimes it is necessary to use notes which are not within the key signature of a piece of music. This is when **accidentals** are used. An accidental is a temporary alteration to the pitch of a note. An accidental may be a sharp, a flat, or a natural. A **natural sign** (shown below) is used to cancel a sharp or flat. Like a sharp or flat, the natural affects all notes of that pitch for the rest of the bar in which it occurs, unless another accidental occurs after it.

The Natural Sign

 46.0

This example demonstrates accidentals applied to the note **G** in the treble staff. Notice that **G♭** is the same note as **F♯** which you already know.

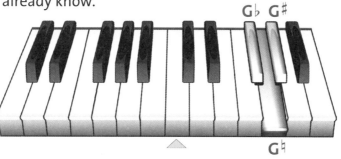

Enharmonic Notes

As you saw in the previous example, the note **G♭** is exactly the same as **F♯**. In music there is often more than one way of naming a note, e.g. **D♯** is the same note as **E♭**, **B♭** is the same note as **A♯**, etc. The different names are called **enharmonic** notes. All the black notes on the piano have more than one name, and white notes can as well, e.g. **E♮** is also **F♭**, and **F♮** is also **E♯**.

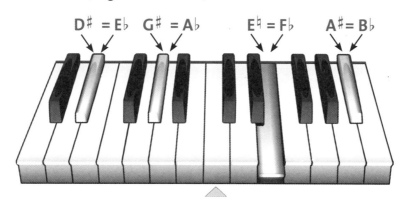

12 Bar Blues

The following piece is an example of the **12 Bar Blues**, which is a musical form central to the **African American** music tradition. It uses a pattern of chords that repeats every 12 bars and may be played in any key. This one contains many accidentals, so take it slowly at first to be sure you are playing the correct notes. Whenever you are learning a melody which contains new notes, play slowly and sing the names of all the notes out loud as you play. Listen carefully as you do this, and try to sing the same pitch as you are playing.

 46.1   **Accidental Blues**

P. Gelling

Blue Notes

In Blues playing, it is common to add notes from outside the major key, and to alter some of the notes to make the overall sound more "bluesy". The most common alterations are the **flattened third** (♭3), the **flattened fifth** (♭5) and the **flattened seventh** (♭7). These are called **Blue notes**, or Blues notes. The first blue note we will examine is the ♭3 which is **E♭** in the key of C. listen to how effective it sounds when alternated with the natural 3rd degree (**E**).

▶ 47.0

▶ 47.1

This example uses the **flattened fifth** (**G♭**) and the **flattened seventh** (**B♭**) along with the flattened 3rd (**E♭**). Notice how effective blue notes sound when combined with harmony notes in bars 3 and 4.
Once you can play this example, try improvising with chord tones and blue notes.

LESSON EIGHTEEN

The Blues Scale

One of the most practical ways of remembering the blue notes is to use the **Blues Scale**. It contains all three of the blue notes: ♭3, ♭5 and ♭7. The Blues scale can be played starting on **any** note. It is shown here in the key of **C**.

 48.0

It is worth comparing the notes of the Blues scale with those of the major scale. Here are the notes of both scales in the key of C.

C MAJOR SCALE							
C	D	E	F	G	A	B	C
1	2	3	4	5	6	7	8

C BLUES SCALE						
C	E♭	F	G♭	G	B♭	C
1	♭3	4	♭5	5	♭7	8

Notice that the Blues scale contains both the flat 5 and the natural 5. It does not contain the degrees 2 or 6. Altogether the Blues scale contains **six** different notes, whereas the major scale contains seven different notes. The major scale used by itself does not sound very bluesy. However, Blues melodies often contain notes from both of these scales. Listen to the following example to hear the difference between them.

 48.1

C Major Scale   C Blues Scale

The following solo will help you become more comfortable with the Blues scale. The scale is played ascending and descending over the three bass notes **C**, **F** and **G** which are $\underline{\text{I}}$, $\underline{\text{IV}}$ and $\underline{\text{V}}$ in the key of C. Notice how changing the bass note alters the sound. Notice also the use of octaves in the left hand part. Practice each hand by itself at first if necessary.

Riffs

In the following example, the right hand plays a **riff** created from the Blues scale. A riff is a short repeating pattern which may be altered to fit various chord changes. Riffs are very common in Blues. Try inventing some of your own.

First and Second Endings

The next song contains **first and second endings**. The **first** time you play through the song, play the **first** ending, (1.   ), then go back to the beginning. The **second** time you play through the song, play the **second** ending (2.   ) instead of the first.

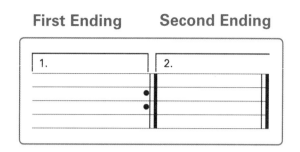

First Ending   Second Ending

LESSON NINETEEN

The Triplet

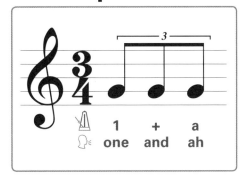

An eighth note triplet is a group of three evenly spaced notes played within 1 beat. Eighth note triplets are indicated by three eighth notes with the number **3** written either above or below the group. Sometimes the triplet has a bracket or a curved line around the number 3. The eighth note triplets are played with a third of a beat each. Triplets are easy to understand once you have heard them played. Listen to the recording if you are unsure of the timing.

▶ 52

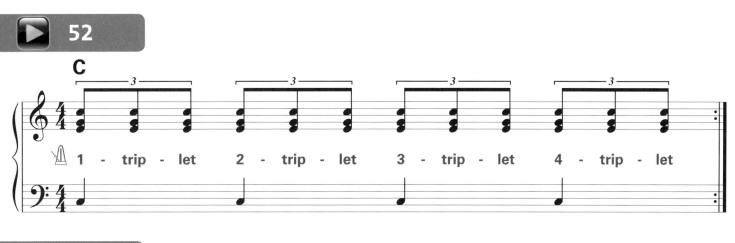

▶ 53

This example uses a constant stream of triplets on the chords played by the right hand.

Here is a 12 Bar Blues pattern which makes use of triplets. Notice the left hand riff in this example where a new note is played on each beat. This is called a walking bass line.

One of the great sounds in Blues is fast single note runs using triplets. The Blues scale is very effective for playing these type of runs. Speed comes with practice, but practice slowly at first and concentrate on accuracy.

The use of repetition with notes from the Blues scale is also a great sound.

LESSON TWENTY

Swing Rhythms

A **swing rhythm** is created by tying together the first two notes of a triplet. There are several different ways of writing swing rhythms. To understand them, it is worth using one musical example written in various ways. The example below has the first and second notes of the triplet group tied together.
Play this example and listen to the feeling created by the rhythm.

Instead of tying the first two notes of the triplet group, a quarter note can be used. The quarter note grouped with an eighth note by a triplet bracket shows clearly that the first note is worth two thirds of the beat, while the second note is worth only one third. Play the following example and notice that it sounds the same as the previous one.

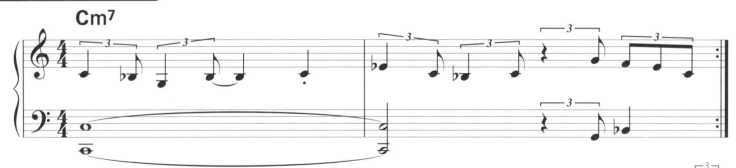

A third way to write the same rhythm is to notate the whole thing in eighth notes and to write ♫ = ♩♪ at the start of the music. Jazz players usually write swing rhythms in this manner as it is easier to read. Play the following example and notice that once again it sounds the same.

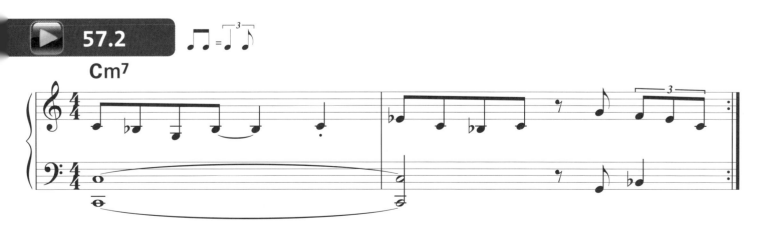

The Shuffle

By playing a constant stream of swinging eighth notes, an effect known as the **Shuffle** can be created. A good way to start coordinating both hands when playing a shuffle is to play the **shuffle rhythm** with the **left hand** and **triplets** with the **right hand**. Both hands coincide on the **first** and **third** part of each triplet.

Here is another shuffle, this time written differently. Notice the use of the 7th of each chord in the left hand part. If you have trouble with this one, practice each hand separately at first.

LESSON TWENTY ONE

Seventh Chords

Chord Symbol **7**

After major and minor, the next most common chord type is the **seventh chord**, (sometimes called the dominant seventh chord). Seventh chords consist of **four notes** taken from the major scale of the same letter name. These notes are the first (**1**), third (**3**), fifth (**5**) and **flattened seventh** (♭**7**) notes of the major scale, so the **chord formula** for the seventh chord is:

1   3   5   ♭7

A flattened seventh (♭**7**) is created by lowering the seventh note of the major scale by one semitone. This is the same ♭**7** note that is found in the Blues scale. Notice that the seventh chord is simply a major chord with a flattened seventh note added.

The G Seventh Chord (G7)

Chord Symbol **G7**

G   B   D   F
1   3   5   ♭7

The **G7** chord can be constructed from the G major scale. Using the seventh chord formula on the G major scale gives the notes **G**, **B**, **D** and **F**. When the seventh note of the G major scale (**F♯**) is flattened, it becomes an **F** natural.

Note Name	G	A	B	C	D	E	♯F	G
Note Number	1	2	3	4	5	6	7	8
Seventh Chord Formula	1		3		5		♭7	
G Seventh Chord	G		B		D		F	

Play the notes of the **G7** chord with the **first**, **second**, **fourth** and **fifth** fingers of your right hand, individually and then together as shown below.

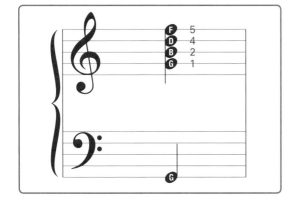

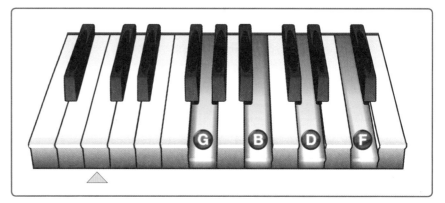

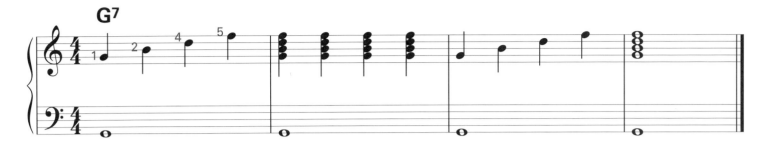

G7 Chord Inversions

Because the **G7** chord contains **four notes**, there are **three inversions** plus the root position. The following three diagrams illustrate the first inversion (3 5 ♭7 1), the second inversion (5 ♭7 1 3), and the third inversion (♭7 1 3 5) of the G7 chord.

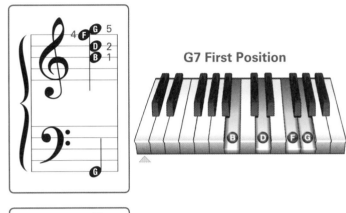

G7 First Position

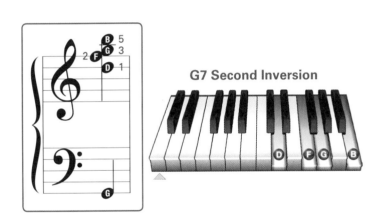

G7 Second Inversion

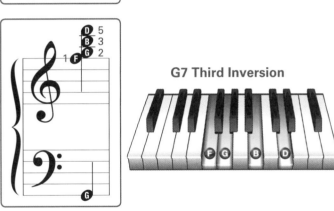

G7 Third Inversion

The example below uses all the inversions of the G7 chord. Use the correct fingerings as shown in the diagrams.

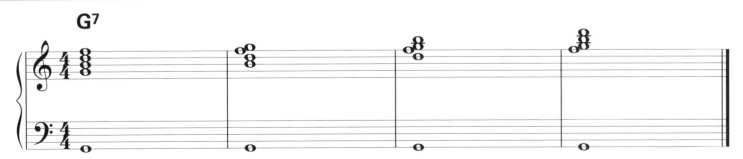

Seventh chords are particularly common in Blues, Boogie and Rock'n' Roll piano playing. The example below demonstrates a 1st inversion **G7** chord played over the left hand pattern you have been using, this time played as straight eighth notes.

The C7 Chord

Like G7, the **C7** chord contains the degrees 1, 3, 5, ♭7. Its notes are C, E, G and B♭.
Here are the four basic positions of the C7 chord.

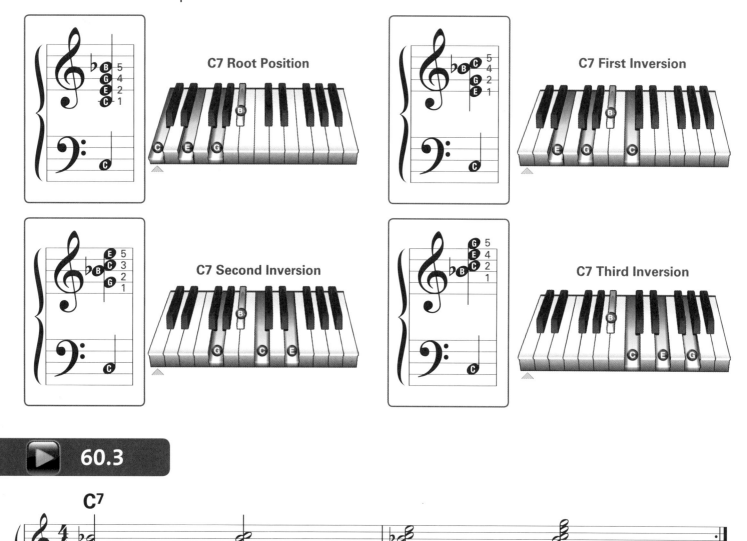

The F7 Chord

Here are the four basic positions for the **F7** chord. Its notes are F, A, C and E♭.

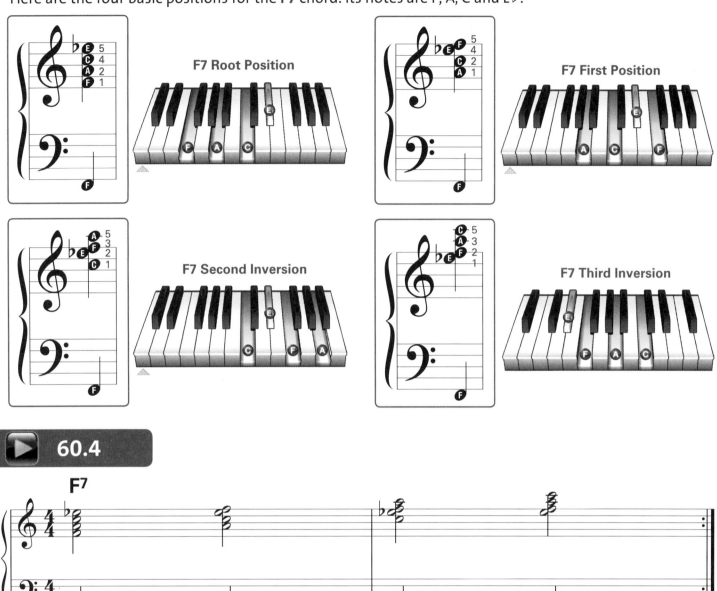

F7 Root Position

F7 First Position

F7 Second Inversion

F7 Third Inversion

▶ **60.4**

F⁷

Omitting Notes from Chords

Because there are four notes in a 7th chord, they are often more difficult to play than major chords. When using 7th chords it is common to leave out one of the notes. The most commonly omitted note is the 5th, although sometimes the 3rd or the root can be omitted. Usually the left hand will be playing the root note anyway. As long as the ♭7 degree is in the chord you still get the effect of a 7th chord. Here are some examples of partial 7th chords.

▶ **60.5**

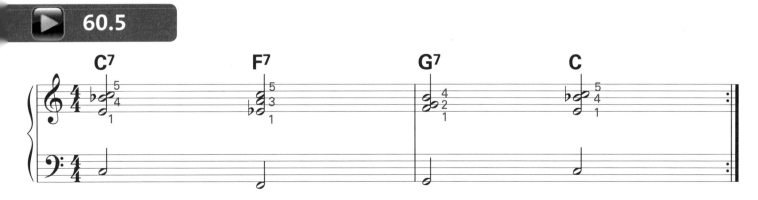

C⁷   F⁷   G⁷   C

Listen to how good these chords sound when applied to a 12 Bar Blues progression. Learn this example and then experiment with different rhythms using the same chords, as well as different inversions using the same rhythms. Feel free to leave out any note other than the ♭7 when using any of the inversions.

LESSON TWENTY TWO

Scale Tone Chords

The example below shows chords built on all the degrees of the **C** major scale. In **any** key it is possible to build chords on each degree of the scale. This means that for every major scale, there are **seven** possible chords which can be used for creating piano parts and harmonizing melodies. These seven chords are called **scale tone chords**. It is common practice to describe chords within a key with **roman numerals** as shown here.

▶ **62.0**

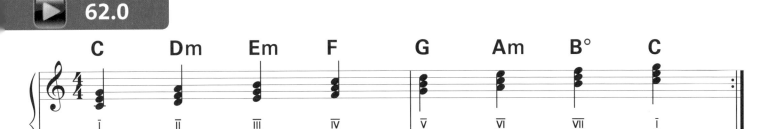

The **B diminished** chord contains the notes **B**, **D** and **F**. Like major and minor chords, it can be played in three inversions which are shown below.

The B Diminished Chord

These three diagrams illustrate the root position (1 ♭3 ♭5), first inversion (♭3 ♭5 1), and second inversion (♭5 1 ♭3) of the **Bdim** chord.

B	D	F
1	♭3	♭5

B°   **B° Chord (Second inversion)**   **Chord Symbol**

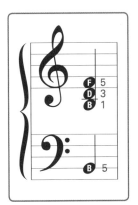

Bdim Root Position

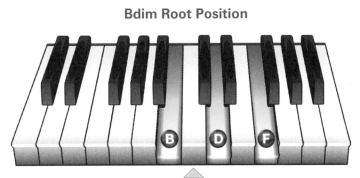

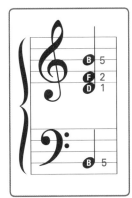

Bdim First Inversion

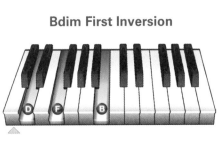

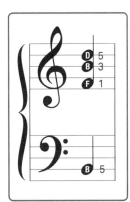

Bdim Second Inversion

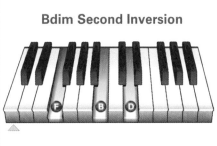

The following example demonstrates the root position, first inversion, second inversion, and an octave of the root position of the Bdim chord.

Using Roman Numerals for Chords

If you look at some simple progressions in the key of C major, it is easy to see how the system of roman numerals works. The following example contains the chords **C**, **F** and **G**. Since these chords correspond to the first, fourth and fifth degrees of the C major scale, the progression could be described as Ī ĪV V̄ Ī in the **key of C.**

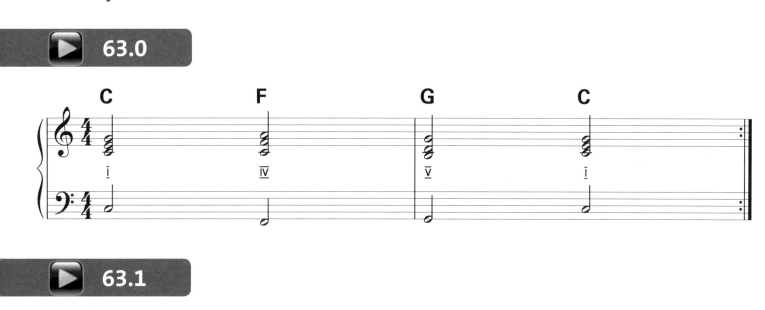

This one contains the chords **C**, **Em**, **Dm** and **G** which correspond to the first, third, second and fifth degrees of the C major scale. Therefore the progression could be described as Ī ĪĪĪ ĪĪ V̄ in the key of C.

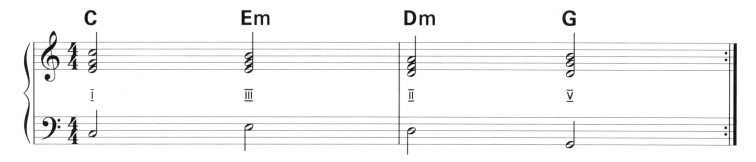

LESSON TWENTY THREE

Using the Sustain Pedal

When moving between chords, it is often necessary to lift one or both hands off the piano completely. This results in a gap in sound between one chord and the next. Sometimes this is desirable, and other times it is not. The use of the **sustain pedal** makes it possible to keep a note or chord sounding while the hands move to a new position.

On a piano, the pedal is part of the instrument itself. There are also other pedals on the piano which vary between upright and grand pianos. For now, we will deal specifically with the sustain pedal. The sustain pedal (also called the **sostenuto** pedal) is always the one to the **right** of the other pedals, because it is operated with the **right foot**. On electronic pianos the sustain pedal is a separate attachment which can be plugged into the socket provided on the back of the piano.

The photos below show the pedals on both upright and grand pianos as well as a sustain pedal for an electronic piano. To hear how the sustain pedal works, play a chord and then press the pedal down with your right foot. Hold the pedal down and lift your hands off the piano - the chord continues to sound as long as the pedal is held down. This makes changing chords a lot easier.

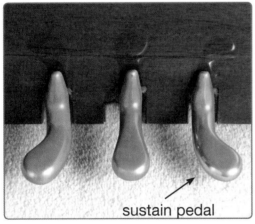

sustain pedal

Upright Piano Pedals

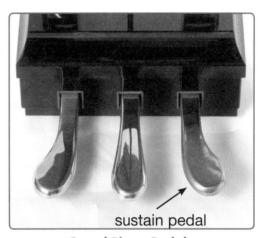

sustain pedal

Grand Piano Pedals

Electronic Piano Pedal

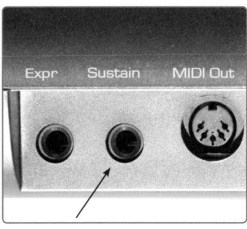

Socket on Back of Piano

The following example demonstrates a typical use of the sustain pedal. In the first two bars, the right hand moves between inversions of a C major chord. Listen to the gap between each chord as the hand is lifted off the piano. In the third and fourth bars, the sustain pedal is pressed down as each new inversion is played. This eliminates the gaps in sound between the chords. The use of the pedal is indicated by the symbol **Ped.**

64.0

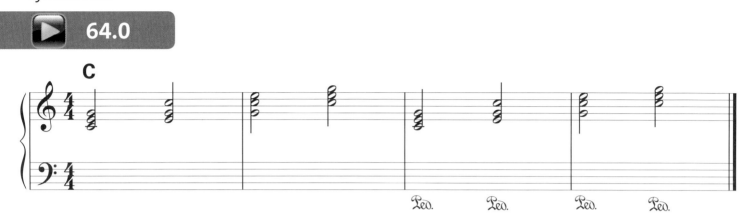

The basic rule when using the sustain pedal is that it must be **released when the harmony changes**. This is demonstrated in the following example. The pedal is held down between bars 1 and 2 while the left hand changes from a **C** chord to a **G7** chord. When the pedal is held down, the first chord blends in with the second chord, causing a clash in harmony and a muddy sound. This is definitely undesirable! In the rest of the example, **the pedal is quickly released as each new chord is struck by the hand and then immediately pressed down again until the next chord is struck**. This is the correct way to use the pedal. Practice this example many times each day until you can co-ordinate it with your hand. Then try playing the chords with the right hand, then both hands.

64.1

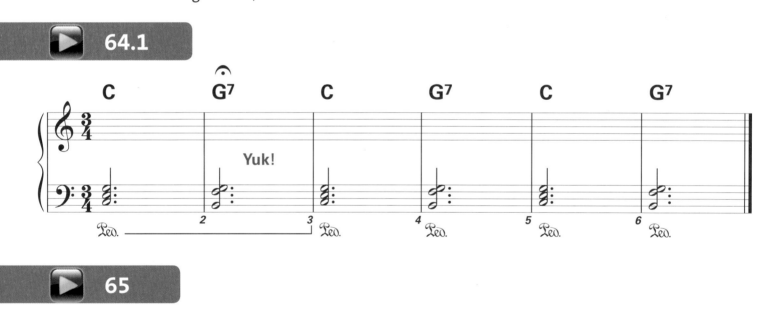

65

In this example, broken chords are played by the right hand. Because all the notes are part of the one harmony, it is not necessary to release the pedal until a new chord is played.

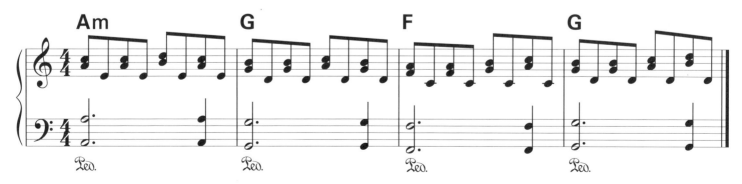

You will often find printed music which doesn't contain pedal markings, so it is up to you to decide where to use the pedal. The best place to pedal is usually where a new chord occurs. In the following examples, the chord changes are indicated with roman numerals. Try pedalling on each chord change.

66

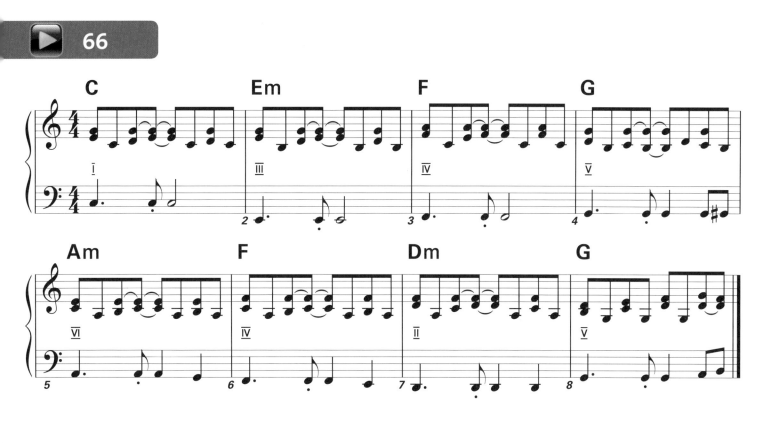

67

This part looks more complex and is harder to play, but it is based on an even simpler underlying chord progression. Once again, you could pedal where the chords change.

Here is a piece which uses all the scale tone chords in the key of **C**. Notice the use of slash chords and passing notes throughout the piece. Don't forget to experiment with using the sustain pedal. Most sheet music doesn't contain pedal markings, as it is left to the player's discretion. The general principle is that the busier the part is rhythmically, the less the pedal is used. No two players pedal exactly the same, so over time you need to develop a method that works best for you.

68   Seven Seas

LESSON TWENTY FOUR

Intervals

An interval is the distance between two musical notes. Intervals are measured in numbers, and are calculated by counting the number of letter names (**A B C D E F G A**) between and including the notes being measured. Within an octave, intervals are: **Unison** (two notes of the same pitch played or sung together or consecutively), **2nd**, **3rd**, **4th**, **5th**, **6th**, **7th** and **Octave** (two notes an octave apart). Thus **A** to **B** is a **2nd** interval, as is B to C, C to D etc. **A** to **C** is a **3rd** interval, **A** to **D** is a **4th**, **A** to **E** is a **5th**, **A** to **F** is a **6th**, **A** to **G** is a **7th** and **A** to the next **A** is an **octave**.

Intervals may be **melodic** (two notes played consecutively) or **harmonic** (two notes played at the same time). Hence two people singing at the same time are said to be singing in harmony.

Interval Qualities

Different intervals have different qualities, as shown below:

Quality	Can be applied to
Perfect	Unisons, 4ths, 5ths and Octaves
Major	2nds, 3rds, 6ths and 7ths
Minor	2nds, 3rds, 6ths and 7ths
Augmented	All intervals
Diminished	All intervals

These intervals can be best explained with the aid of a chromatic scale. If you look at the one below, it is easy to see that since intervals are measured in semitones, they may begin or end on a sharp or flat rather than a natural note.

4ths, 5ths and **octaves** are **perfect** intervals because they cannot be major or minor. If you **widen** a perfect interval by a semitone it becomes **augmented** (added to). E.g. if you add a semitone to the perfect 4th interval **C** to **F**, it becomes the **augmented 4th interval C** to **F♯**. Notice that the letter name remains the same—it is not referred to as C to G♭.

If you narrow a perfect interval by a semitone they become **diminished** (lessened). E.g. if you lessen the perfect 5th interval **D** to **A** by a semitone, it becomes the **diminished 5th interval D** to **A♭**. Again, the letter name remains the same—it is not referred to as D to G♯.

Major intervals (2nds, 3rds, 6ths and 7ths) become minor if narrowed by a semitone and **minor** intervals become major if widened by a semitone. A **diminished** interval can be created by narrowing a perfect or minor interval by a semitone. An **augmented** interval can be created by widening a perfect or major interval by a semitone.

    www.learntoplaymusic.com

Interval Distances

In summary, here is a list of the distances of all common intervals up to an octave, measured in semitones. Each new interval is one semitone wider apart than the previous one. Notice that the interval of an octave is exactly twelve semitones. This is because there are twelve different notes in the chromatic scale. Notice also that the interval which has a distance of six semitones can be called either an augmented 4th or a diminished 5th. This interval is also often called a **tritone** (6 semitones = 3 tones).

> **Minor 2nd** - One semitone
>
> **Major 2nd** - Two semitones
>
> **Minor 3rd** - Three semitones
>
> **Major 3rd** - Four semitones
>
> **Perfect 4th** - Five semitones
>
> **Augmented 4th or Diminished 5th** - Six semitones
>
> **Perfect 5th** - Seven semitones
>
> **Minor 6th** - Eight semitones
>
> **Major 6th** - Nine semitones
>
> **Minor 7th** - Ten semitones
>
> **Major 7th** - Eleven semitones
>
> **Perfect Octave** - Twelve semitones

The following example demonstrates all of the common intervals ascending within one octave starting and ending on the note **C**.

Chord Construction

Chords are usually made up of combinations of major and minor third intervals. All of the chords you have learnt up to this point have been **triads** (3 note chords). There are **four** basic types of triads: **major**, **minor**, **augmented** and **diminished**. Examples of each of these triads are shown below along with the formula for each one.

C Major Chord

C Minor Chord

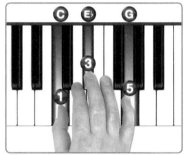

C Augmented Chord

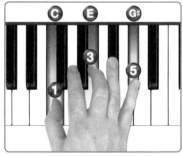

C Diminished Chord

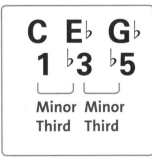

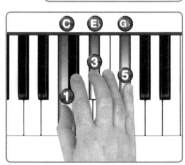

This example demonstrates the four basic types of triads shown on the previous page.

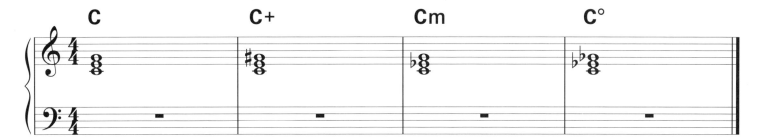

All types of chords can be played in different positions on the piano in various inversions. This example demonstrates how the four basic triad types could be used in a more musical manner. The right hand plays voicings which are close together on the piano, while the left hand outlines each chord as an arpeggio starting from the root.

Scale Tone Chords in G

By using the correct formulas, it is possible to build any of the four types of triads on any note of the chromatic scale. E.g. if you start with the note D and add a note a major third above it (F♯) and a minor third above that (A), you end up with a D major chord. If you start with the note A and add a note a minor third above it (C) and a major third above that (E), you end up with an A minor chord.

If you go through and analyse all of the scale tone chords in the key of C major, you end up with the following pattern:

I	**Major**	(C Major)
II	**Minor**	(D Minor)
III	**Minor**	(E Minor)
IV	**Major**	(F Major)
V	**Major**	(G Major)
VI	**Minor**	(A Minor)
VII	**Diminished**	(B Diminished)

This pattern remains the same regardless of the key. This means that if you look at the scale tone triads in **any major key**, chord I is **always** major, chord II is always minor, chord III is always minor, etc. The only thing that changes from one key to the next is the letter names of the chords. This can be demonstrated by looking at the scale tone triads for the key of **G major** which are shown below.

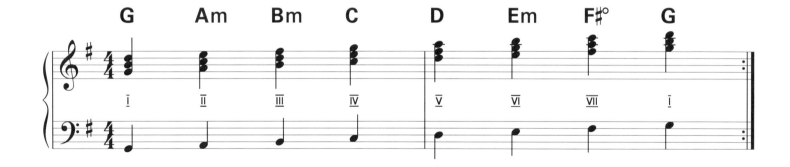

LESSON TWENTY FIVE

How to Transpose

Transposing (or transposition) means changing the key of a piece of music. By using the system of roman numerals it is very easy to transpose a chord progression from one key to another. The same system is also useful for communicating progressions and parts to other musicians.

The example below shows a simple piano part in the key of C, based on the chords C, F and G. This progression can be described as Ī IV̄ V̄.

▶ 73.0

▶ 73.1

To transpose the above part to the key of G, you need to know chords Ī IV̄ V̄ in that key (G, C and D). Here is the same part transposed to the key of G.

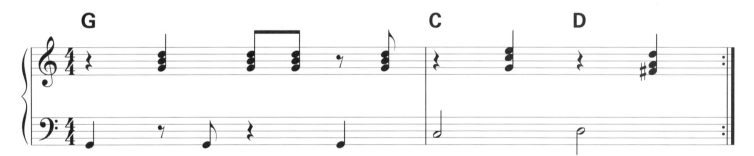

New Chords in the Key of G

The above example contains the chord **D major** which you have not previously learnt. By using the chord construction formulas from the previous lesson, you can easily work out that a **D chord** contains the notes **D**, **F♯** and **A**. Like any chord, there is more than one way to play a D chord. The diagrams on the following page show the D chord in root position, first inversion and second inversion.

D Major Chord Inversions

These three diagrams illustrate the root position (1 3 5), first inversion (3 5 1), and second inversion (5 1 3) of the **D** chord.

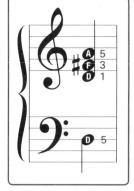

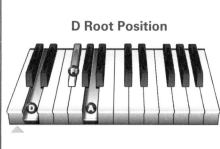

D Root Position

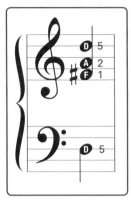

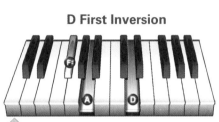

D First Inversion

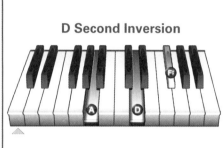

D Second Inversion

 74.0

The key of G also contains the chords **B minor** and **F♯ diminished**. In the following diagrams, these chords are shown in root position, first inversion and second inversion.

B Minor Chord Inversions

These three diagrams illustrate the root position (1 ♭3 5), first inversion (♭3 5 1), and second inversion (5 1 ♭3) of the **Bm** chord.

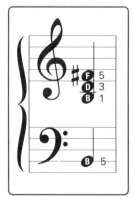

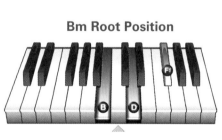

Bm Root Position

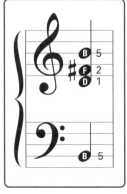

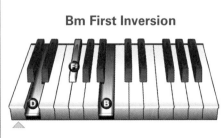

Bm First Inversion

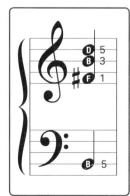

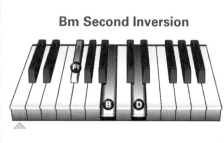

Bm Second Inversion

This example contains all three inversions of the **Bm** chord.

F♯ Diminished Chord Inversions

These three diagrams illustrate the root position (1 ♭3 ♭5), first inversion (♭3 ♭5 1), and second inversion (♭5 1 ♭3) of the **F♯** dim chord

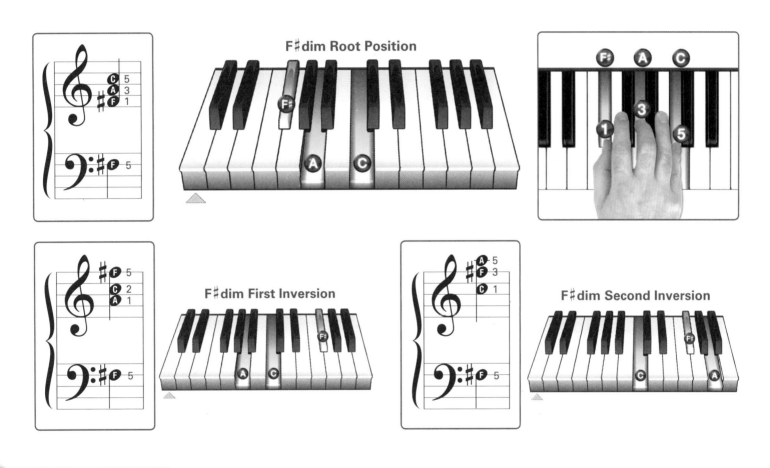

F♯dim Root Position

F♯dim First Inversion

F♯dim Second Inversion

F♯°

Here is a piano part which makes use of the chords **Bm** and **F♯dim**.

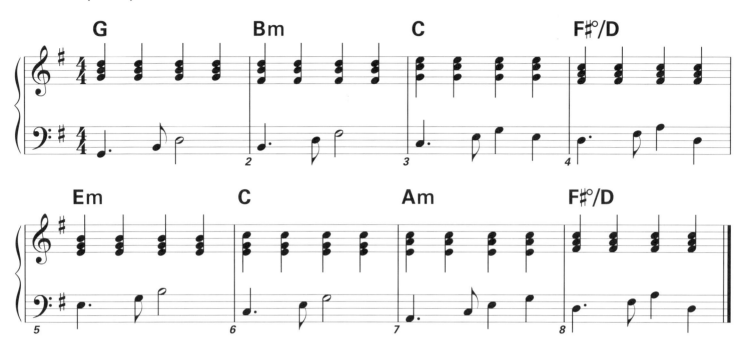

Like any piece of music, the above example can be transposed to other keys. Here is the same part in the key of **C**.

LESSON TWENTY SIX

Minor Scales and Keys

Apart from major keys, the other basic tonality used in western music is a **minor key**. Minor keys are often said to have a sadder or darker sound than major keys. Songs in a minor key use notes taken from a **minor scale**. There are three types of minor scale – the **natural minor scale**, the **harmonic minor scale** and the **melodic minor scale**. Written below is the **A natural minor** scale. It contains exactly the same notes as the C major scale. The difference is that it starts and finishes on an **A** note instead of a C note. The A note then becomes the key note. The A natural minor scale is easy to learn – it is simply the notes of the **musical alphabet**.

A Natural Minor Scale	A	B	C	D	E	F	G	A	
C Major Scale			C	D	E	F	G	A	B	C

 77   A Natural Minor Scale

Here is the A natural minor scale played with both hands – first in eighth notes over two octaves and then in sixteenth notes over three octaves.

Tempo Changes

There are specific markings for changes in tempo. The most common ones are listed below.
Notice the use of the **rit.** marking near the end of the following song.

accelerando (gradually becoming faster)

ritenuto (rit) (immediately slower)

rallentando/ ritardando (gradually becoming slower)

a tempo (return to the original tempo)

The melody of this traditional Christmas song is derived from the natural minor scale. Because of this, it is said to be in a **minor key**. It is written here in the key of **A minor**.

 78 God Rest Ye Merry Gentlemen

www.learntoplaymusic.com

Relative Major and Minor Keys

Look at the song on the previous page, and notice that although the previous piece is in the key of **A minor**, all the chords it contains are also in the key of C major. For every key signature there are two possible keys, one major and one minor. These are called **relative** keys, e.g. the key signature for the key of C major contains **no sharps or flats**, as does the key of A minor. The key of A minor is therefore called the **relative minor** of C major.

The key signatures for **C major** and **A minor** are identical - no sharps or flats.

To find the relative minor of any major key, start on the 6th degree of the major scale. The example below shows the scale tone chords for the key of A natural minor. Notice that the chords are exactly the same as those contained in the key of C major. The only difference is the starting and finishing point. Because the minor scale starts on **A**, A minor will now be chord ī instead of v̄ī.

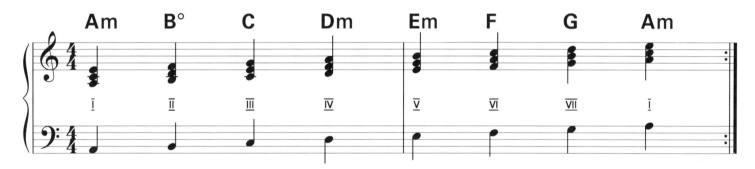

The following progression could be described in two possible ways. It could be called v̄ī v̄ v̄ī v̄ī v̄ in **C major** or ī v̄īī ī v̄ī v̄īī in **A minor**. Because the progression has an obvious minor sounding tonality, musicians would use the second description. Experiment with other chord combinations in the key of A minor.

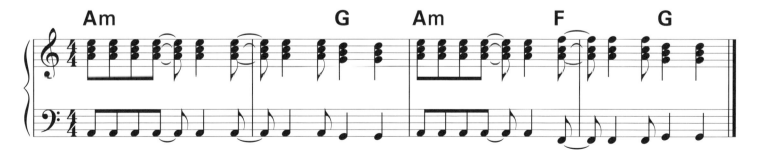

Written below are the scale tone chords for the key of **E natural minor** which is the relative minor of **G** major, as shown by the key signature. As with the keys of C major and A minor, the chords will be the same as those of its relative, but the starting note is **E** instead of G, so **E minor** will be chord ī.

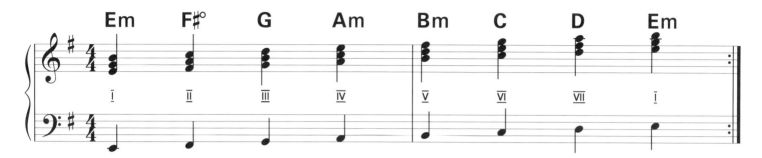

Like music written in major keys, anything in a minor key can be transposed to other keys.
The following example shows the piano part from example 80 transposed to the key of **E minor**.

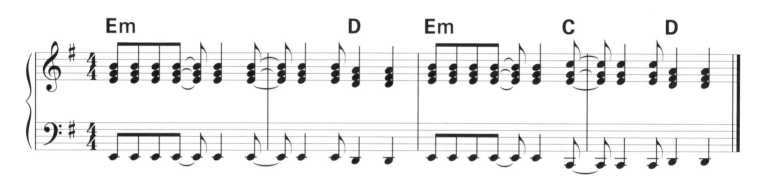

Sometimes only two chords are needed to give the effect of a minor key. Notice also the use of space in this piano part. Particularly when playing with other instruments, it is not necessary to play all the time. Try transposing this part to the key of A minor.

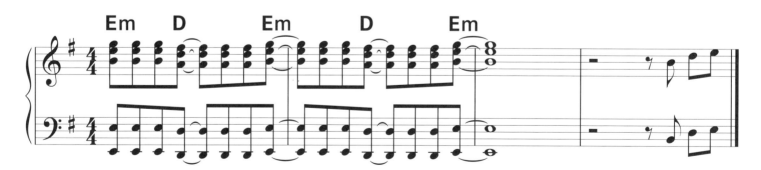

LESSON TWENTY SEVEN

More About Minor Keys and Scales

For every minor key, there are three basic types of minor scale—the **natural minor scale**, the **harmonic minor scale** and the **melodic minor scale**. Each has its own pattern of tones and semitones, as can be seen in the three A minor scales below. The degrees of each scale are written under the note names.

▶ 84.0   A Natural Minor

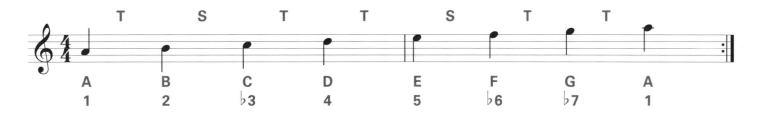

▶ 84.1   A Harmonic Minor

Notice the distance of 1½ tones (three semitones) between the 6th and 7th degrees of the harmonic minor scale. This scale is often described as having an "Eastern" sound.

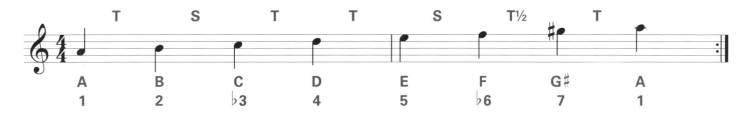

▶ 84.2   A Melodic Minor

In the **A melodic minor** scale, the **6th** and **7th** notes are sharpened when ascending and return to natural when descending. This is the way the melodic minor is used in Classical music. However, in Jazz and other modern styles, the melodic minor descends the same way as it ascends. An easy way to think of the ascending melodic minor is as a major scale with a flattened third degree.

The Harmonic Minor Scale

The raised 7th in the harmonic minor is not indicated in the key signature; instead it is shown as an accidental each time it occurs. In the key of A minor, all the notes are naturals except for the raised 7th degree, which is a **G♯**. The following example demonstrates two octaves of the A harmonic minor scale with each hand. The fingering is the same as that of the A natural minor scale.

 85   **A Harmonic Minor**

Harmonic Minor Scale Tone Chords

Because there are three different minor scales, it is possible to come up with different sets of chords for a minor key by building chords on the notes of each different minor scale. Each variation to the notes of the scale alters the type of chords built on the scale. The letter names of the chords remain the same, but the chord type may change. E.g. shown below are scale tone chords derived from the **A harmonic minor scale**. Notice that chord IIĪ is now **augmented (C+)** instead of major, and also that chord V̄ is **major (E)** instead of minor and chord V̄IĪ is **diminished (G♯°)** instead of major. These changes are all brought about by the raising of the 7th degree of the scale from **G** to **G♯**. The new chords are shown below in root position.

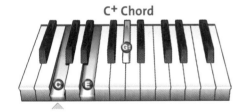

C+ Chord

E Chord

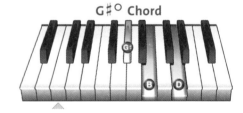

G♯° Chord

 86

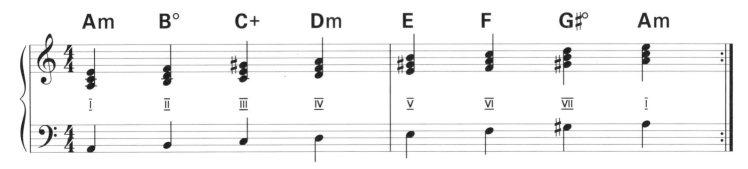

Here is a piece derived from the A harmonic minor scale and its scale tone triads.

Like all chords, the scale tone chords derived from the harmonic minor scale can be arranged into inversions. Here are the inversions of the **E major** chord.

The Melodic Minor Scale

The ascending melodic minor scale contains raised **6th and 7th** degrees, neither of which appear in the key signature. In the key of A minor, these notes are **F♯** and **G♯**. Both notes are notated as accidentals. The following example demonstrates two octaves of the A melodic minor scale with each hand. Remember that the 7th and 6th degrees fall by a semitone when the scale descends.

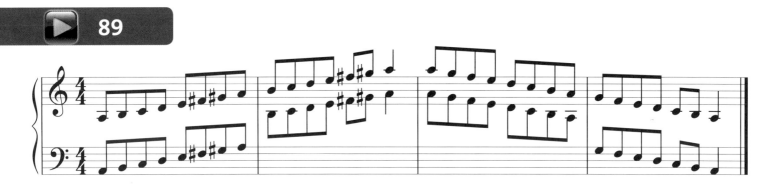

Melodic Minor Scale Tone Chords

The scale tone chords derived from the **A melodic minor scale** are shown below. Because of the sharpened 6th degree, there will be more changes to the types of chords derived from this scale. Chord II is now **minor (Bm)** instead of major, chord IV is **major (D)** instead of minor and chord VI is **diminished (F♯dim)** instead of major. These changes are all brought about by the raising of the 6th degree of the scale from **F** to **F♯**.

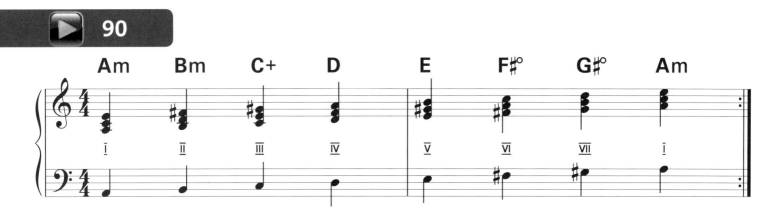

The Six Eight Time Signature

This is the **six eight** time signature.
There are six eighth notes in one bar of 6/8 time.
The six eighth notes are divided into two groups
of three.

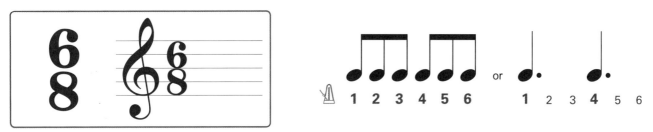

When playing 6/8 time, there are **two** beats within each bar, with each beat being a **dotted quarter note**. Note that this is different from 4/4 and 3/4 time, where each beat is a quarter note. **Accent** (play louder) the 1 and 4 count to help establish the two beats per bar.

When playing music in minor keys, it is common to use chords from all three types of minor scales. A good example of this is the song **House of the Rising Sun**. Look through the chords and see which ones come from each type of minor scale.

LESSON TWENTY EIGHT

The Minor Pentatonic Scale

So far all of the piano parts you have learnt have been based on chords and arpeggios. This is important because chords form the harmonic foundation of music. However, there are many parts based on scales instead of chords. A particularly useful scale is the **minor pentatonic** scale which is shown below in the key of A minor. This scale is used for many bass lines as well as being commonly used for soloing and improvisation. Whereas the major and natural minor scales contain seven different notes, pentatonic scales contain only **five**. The minor pentatonic scale can be thought of as a natural minor scale with the second and sixth degrees left out. The notes of the A minor pentatonic scale are **A C D E** and **G**.

 92.0

The following example shows how the A minor pentatonic scale can be used over a chord progression in the key of A minor.

 92.1

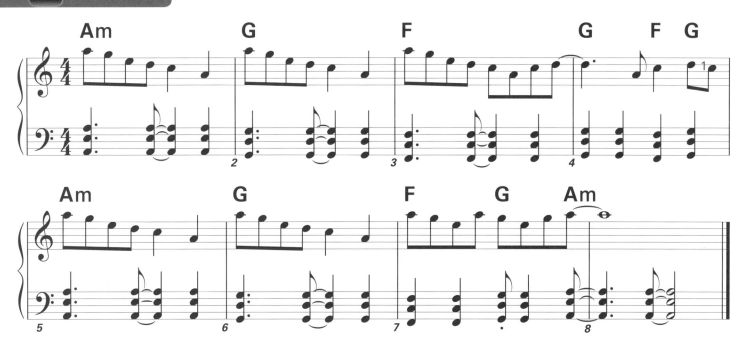

93.0

Here is another example of a riff created from the minor pentatonic scale. This time the right hand plays a line which answers the left hand riff and then plays the riff along with the left hand.

Here are some more piano parts created from the minor pentatonic scale.

93.1

93.2

This example contains a pattern where three notes of the A minor pentatonic scale are played by each hand in contrary motion. Try experimenting with other similar patterns. Notice that both parts are written in the treble staff for this example.

The following left hand pattern is great for improvising over. Practice the left hand by itself, then try playing some chords or pentatonic scale lines over it with the right hand, as shown below.

94.0

94.1

94.2

Minor Pentatonic Scale in E

Like all scales, the minor pentatonic scale can be transposed to any key. Here is the **E** minor pentatonic scale.

Now try this example which is created entirely from the E minor pentatonic scale.

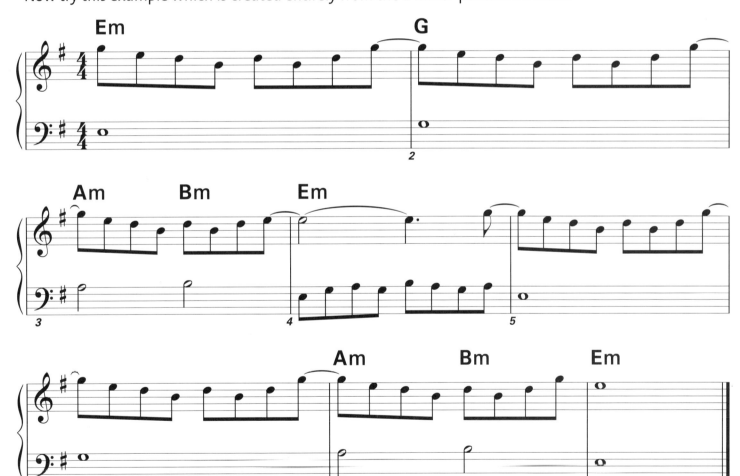

Here is a 12 Bar Blues which uses the E minor pentatonic scale to create lines over the left hand pattern from the previous lesson. Practice each hand separately if necessary.

LESSON TWENTY NINE

Alternating Octaves

Another useful technique in Rock piano playing is the use of alternating octaves with the left hand. Written below is the **E natural minor** scale played in alternating octaves by the **5th** and **1st** fingers of the left hand.

 97.0

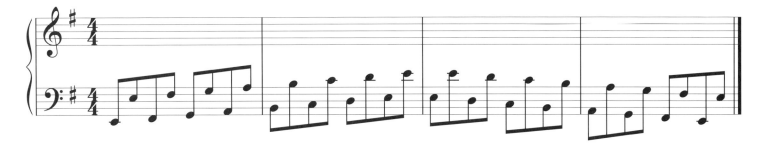

 97.1

Here is a piano part using alternating octaves. It will probably sound familiar to you.

 97.2

This example shows the same part transposed to the key of **A minor**.

Using octaves on repeated notes is a great way to create a driving rhythm. The following 12 Bar Blues shows chords played over an alternating octave left hand part. Take it slowly at first and practice each hand separately if necessary.

Here is another solo which uses an alternating octave left hand part. Co-ordinating the two hands may be difficult at first, so practice each hand separately if necessary. Once you can play it, try using the ideas and techniques to improvise with the right hand. You could also transpose the whole thing to A minor. The more you transpose and improvise with everything you learn, the more confident you will be in your piano knowledge and your ability to play with other musicians. Your eventual aim should be to be able to play any song or short piece you know in **any key**, and improvise on it. All good musicians can do this.

APPENDICES

Notes on the Piano

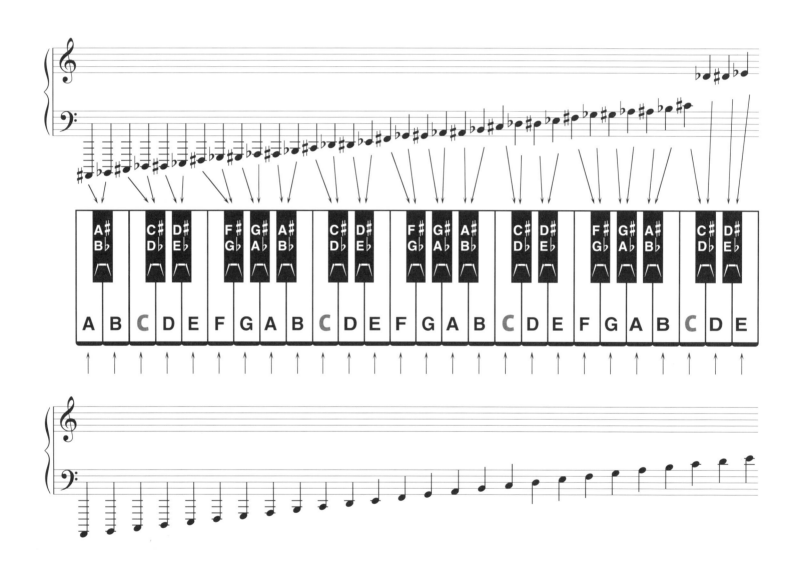

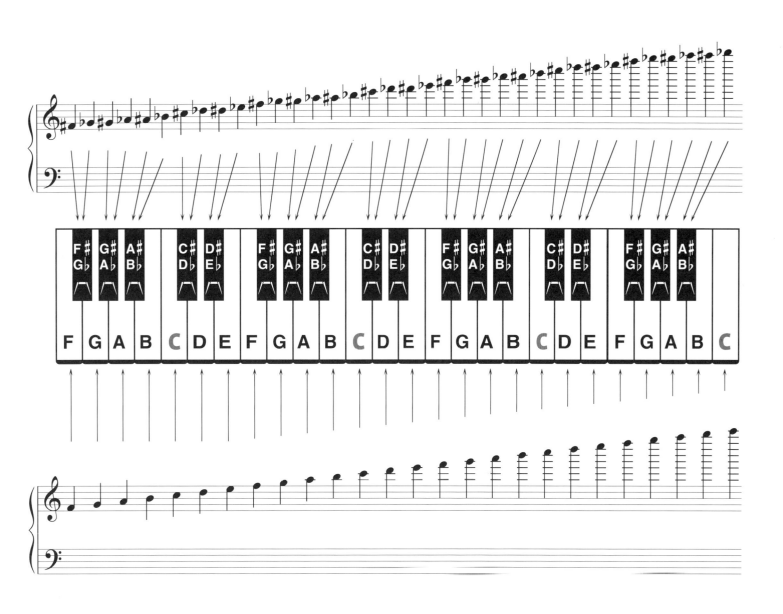

Written below is a summary of all major scales and key signatures.

Major Scales and Key Signatures

Key	#'s/♭'s	Key Signature	Scale
C	0		
G	F♯		
D	F♯ C♯		
A	F♯ C♯ G♯		
E	F♯ C♯ G♯ D♯		
B	F♯ C♯ G♯ D♯ A♯		
F♯	F♯ C♯ G♯ D♯ A♯ E♯		

Major Scales and Key Signatures (cont.)

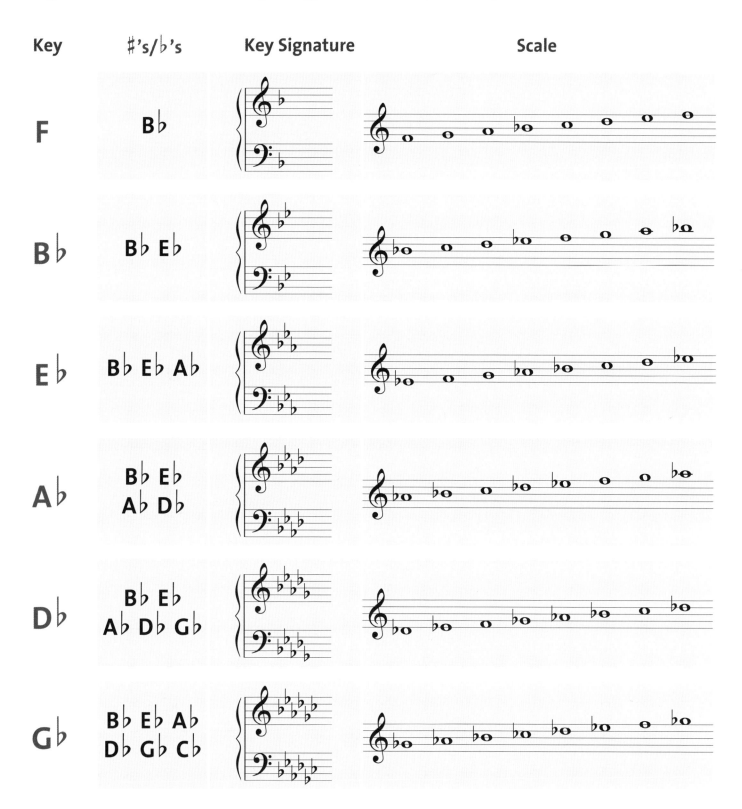

Key	♯'s/♭'s	Key Signature	Scale

It can be seen that each key signature is a shorthand representation of the scale, showing only the sharps or flats which occur in that scale. Where an additional sharp or flat occurs, it is not included as part of the key signature, but is written in the music, e.g. in the **key of G**, if a **D♯** note occurs, the sharp sign will be written immediately before the **D** note, **not** at the beginning of the line as part of the key signature.

Cycle of Fifths

All the major scales can be summarised in the following diagram known as the **Cycle of Fifths** (or the Cycle of Fourths).

Cycle of Fifths

If you start at the top of the cycle, **C**, and go in a clockwise direction, each new key and each new sharp is a fifth higher than the previous key or sharp. The key of **F♯** contains six sharps. After **F♯**, the next logical key would be **C♯** (containing seven sharps). However, this is not practical, and rather than using the key of **C♯**, you would use the enharmonic name for this key, **D♯** (which contains five flats).

Cycle of Fourths

If you start at the top of the cycle, **C**, and go in a counter clockwise direction, each new key and each new flat is a fourth higher than the previous key or flat. The key of **G♭** contains six flats. After **G♭**, the next logical key would be **C♭** (containing seven flats). However, this is not practical, and rather than using the key of **C♭**, you would use the enharmonic name for this key, **B** (which contains five sharps).

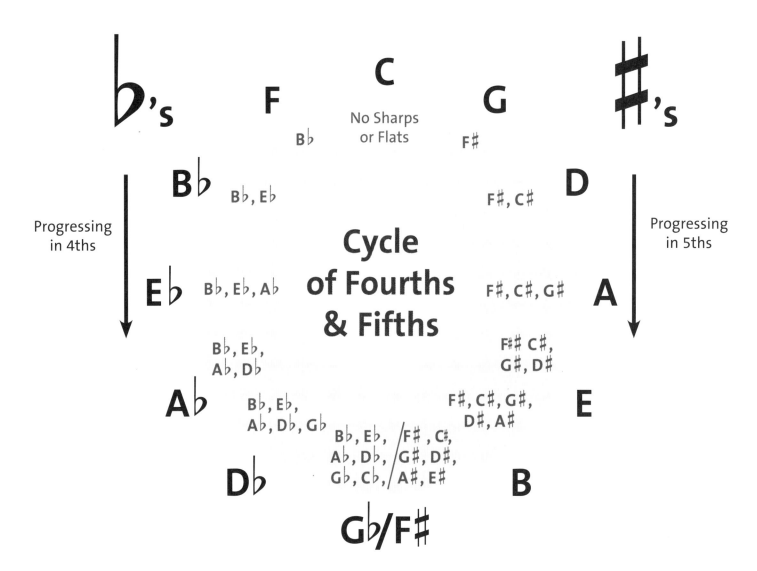

Major Scale Chart

Note's Position in Scale	1	2	3	4	5	6	7	8	9	10	11	12	13
Scale ↓													
A	A	B	C♯	D	E	F♯	G♯	A	B	C♯	D	E	F♯
A♭	A♭	B♭	C	D♭	E♭	F	G	A♭	B♭	C	D♭	E♭	F
B	B	C♯	D♯	E	F♯	G♯	A♯	B	C♯	D♯	E	F♯	G♯
B♭	B♭	C	D	E♭	F	G	A	B♭	C	D	E♭	F	G
C	C	D	E	F	G	A	B	C	D	E	F	G	A
C♯	C♯	D♯	E♯	F♯	G♯	A♯	B♯	C♯	D♯	E♯	F♯	G♯	A♯
D	D	E	F♯	G	A	B	C♯	D	E	F♯	G	A	B
D♭	D♭	E♭	F	G♭	A♭	B♭	C	D♭	E♭	F	G♭	A♭	B♭
E	E	F♯	G♯	A	B	C♯	D♯	E	F♯	G♯	A	B	C♯
E♭	E♭	F	G	A♭	B♭	C	D	E♭	F	G	A♭	B♭	C
F	F	G	A	B♭	C	D	E	F	G	A	B♭	C	D
F♯	F♯	G♯	A♯	B	C♯	D♯	E♯	F♯	G♯	A♯	B	C♯	D♯
G	G	A	B	C	D	E	F♯	G	A	B	C	D	E
G♭	G♭	A♭	B♭	C♭	D♭	E♭	F	G♭	A♭	B♭	C♭	D♭	E♭

Blues Scale Summary

The Blues scale consists of the **1** ♭**3** **4** ♭**5** **5** ♭**7** notes of the major scale. Written below is a summary of all Blues scales.

C Blues Scale

F Blues Scale

G Blues Scale

B♭ Blues Scale

D Blues Scale

E♭ Blues Scale

A Blues Scale

A♭ Blues Scale

E Blues Scale

D♭ Blues Scale

B Blues Scale

G♭ Blues Scale

F♯ Blues Scale

Minor Keys

Many songs are written in a **minor key**. Songs in a minor key use notes taken from a minor scale. There are three types of minor scale — the natural minor scale, the harmonic minor scale and the melodic minor scale. Written below are the three A minor scales, each having its own pattern of tones and semitones.

A Natural Minor

A Harmonic Minor

A Melodic Minor

In the **A melodic minor** scale, the **6th** and **7th** notes are sharpened when ascending and returned to natural when descending.

The most common minor scale in popular music styles is the natural minor scale.

If you compare the **A natural minor** scale with the **C major** scale, you will notice that they contain the same notes (except that they start on different notes). Because of this, these two scales are referred to as being 'relatives'; **A minor** is the **relative minor** of **C major** and vice versa.

For every major scale (and every major chord) there is a relative minor, as listed in the table below.

Major Key	C	D♭	D	E♭	E	F	F♯	G	A♭	A	B♭	B
Relative Minor Key	Am	B♭m	Bm	Cm	C♯m	Dm	D♯m	Em	Fm	F♯m	Gm	G♯m

PROGRESSIVE PIANO FOR ADULTS

To determine whether a song is in a major key or the relative minor key, look at the last note or chord of the song. Songs often finish on the root note or the root chord. E.g., if the key signature contained one sharp, and the last chord of the song was **Em**, the key would probably be **E minor**, not **G major**.

Minor Scales and Key Signatures

Minor Key	Relative Major Key	#'s / ♭'s	Key Signature	Scale
Am	C	0		
Em	G	F#		
Bm	D	F# C#		
F#m	A	F# C# G#		
C#m	E	F# C# G# D#		
G#m	B	F# C# G# D# A#		
D#m	F#	F# C# G# D# A# E#		

Minor Scales and Key Signatures (cont.)

Minor Key	Relative Major Key	♯'s/ ♭'s	Key Signature	Scale

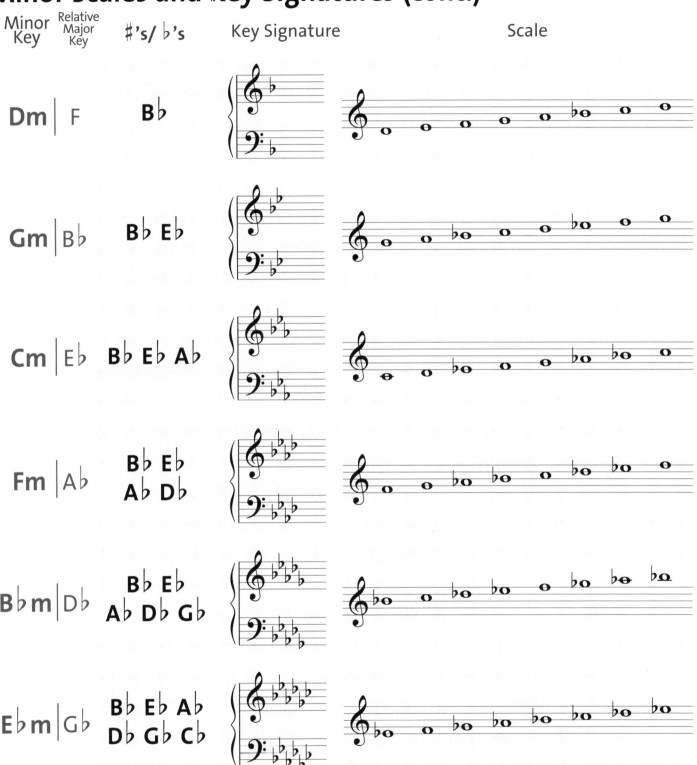

Chord Construction
The Major Chord

A chord can be defined as a group of three or more different notes played together. Every chord is based upon a specific formula which relates back to the major scale after which it is named. The formula for a major chord is **1 3 5**, hence the **C major** chord consists of the first, third and fifth notes of the **C major** scale, i.e. **C–E–G**.

C Major Scale

| Chord Formula | 1 | 3 | 5 |
| Notes | C | E | G |

A chord must contain at least three notes, and any of these three may be repeated. In the **F** chord illustrated there are two **F** notes, one **A** note and one **C** note.

Now consider the **D major** chord, which is constructed from the **D major** scale:

D E F♯ G A B C♯ D

The same formula applies, **1 3 5** major chord formula to the scales outlined on pages 124 and 125 gives the following chord notes:

Chord Name	NOTES IN THE CHORD		
	1(Root Note)*	3	5
C	C	E	G
G	G	B	D
D	D	F♯	A
A	A	C♯	E
E	E	G♯	B
B	B	D♯	F♯
F♯	F♯	A♯	C♯
F	F	A	C
B♭	B♭	D	F
E♭	E♭	G	B♭
A♭	A♭	C	E♭
D♭	D♭	F	A♭
G♭	G♭	B♭	D♭

*The **root note** is the note after which the chord is named (e.g. **C** is the root note of the **C** major chord).

The Minor Chord

The formula for minor chords is **1 ♭3 5**, where ♭3 indicates that the third note of the scale is flattened. It must be remembered that this formula, although used to construct a minor chord, is still based upon the notes of the **major scale**. Thus the **C** minor chord consists of the first, flattened third and fifth notes of the **C major** scale:

C Major Scale

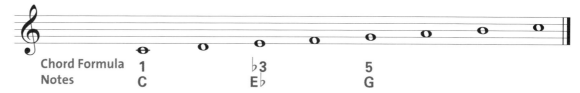

Chord Formula	**1**	**♭3**	**5**
Notes	**C**	**E♭**	**G**

These notes are illustrated in the **C** minor chord below:

The following table lists all of the notes of the minor chords for the scales previously studied:

Chord Name	NOTES IN THE CHORD		
	1(Root Note)	♭3	5
Cm	C	E♭	G
Gm	G	B♭	D
Dm	D	F	A
Am	A	C	E
Em	E	G	B
Bm	B	D	F♯
F♯m	F♯	A	C♯
Fm	F	A	C
B♭m	B♭	D♭	F
E♭m	E♭	G♭	B♭
A♭m	A♭	C♭(B♮)	E♭
D♭m	D♭	F♭(E♮)	A♭
G♭m	G♭	B♭♭*(A♮)	D♭

*A **double flat** (♭♭) lowers the note's pitch by **one tone** e.g. **B♭♭** = **A**.

The Seventh Chord

The seventh chord is formed by adding a flattened 7th note to the major chord.

1 3 5 ♭7

Thus the **C7** chord consists of the first, third, fifth and flattened seventh notes of the **C** major scale

C Major Scale			
Chord Formula	1	3	5	♭7
Notes	C	E	G	B♭

These notes are illustrated in the **C7** chord below:

The following table lists all of the notes of the 7th chords for the scales previously discussed.

	NOTES IN THE CHORD			
Chord Name	**1**	**3**	**5**	**♭7**
C7	C	E	G	B♭
G7	G	B	D	F
D7	D	F♯	A	C
A7	A	C♯	E	G
E7	E	G♯	B	D
B7	B	D♯	F♯	A
F♯7	F♯	A♯	C♯	E
F7	F	A	C	E♭
B♭7	B♭	D	F	A♭
E♭7	E♭	G	B♭	D♭
A♭7	A♭	C	E♭	G♭
D♭7	D♭	F	A♭	C♭ (B♮)
G♭7	G♭	B♭	D♭	F♭ (E♮)

Chord Formula Charts

The following chart gives a comprehensive list of chord formulas, together with an example based on the **C Scale**:

CHORD NAME	CHORD FORMULA	EXAMPLE	
Major	1 3 5	C:	C E G
Suspended	1 4 5	Csus:	C F G
Major add Ninth	1 3 5 9	Cadd9:	C E G D
Minor	1 ♭3 5	Cm:	C E♭ G
Augmented	1 3 ♯5	Caug:	C E G♯
Major Sixth	1 3 5 6	C6:	C E G A
Major Sixth add Ninth	1 3 5 6 9	C6/9:	C E G A D
Minor Sixth	1 ♭3 5 6	Cm6:	C E♭ G A
Minor Sixth add Ninth	1 ♭3 5 6 9	Cm6/9:	C E♭ G A D
Seventh	1 3 5 ♭7	C7:	C E G B♭
Seventh Suspended	1 4 5 ♭7	C7sus:	C F G B♭
Minor Seventh	1 ♭3 5 ♭7	Cm7:	C E♭ G B♭
Diminished Seventh	1 ♭3 5 ♭♭7	Cdim	C E♭ G♭ B♭♭ (A)
Major Seventh	1 3 5 7	Cmaj7:	C E G B
Minor Major Seventh	1 ♭3 5 7	Cm(maj7):	C E♭ G B
Ninth	1 3 5 ♭7 9	C9:	C E G B♭ D
Minor Ninth	1 ♭3 5 ♭7 9	Cm9:	C E♭ G B♭ D
Major Ninth	1 3 5 7 9	Cmaj9:	C E G B D
Eleventh	1 3* 5 ♭7 9 11	C11:	C E* G B♭ D F
Minor Eleventh	1 ♭3 5 ♭7 9 11	Cm11:	C E♭ G B♭ D F
Thirteenth	1 3 5 7 9 11* 13	C13:	C E G B♭ D F* A
Minor Thirteenth	1 ♭3 5 ♭7 9 11* 13	Cm13:	C E♭ G B♭ D F* A

*indicates that a note is optional.

A **double flat** ♭♭, lowers the note's pitch by **one tone**.
A **double sharp** ✕, raises the note's pitch by **one tone**.

Scale Tone Chords

In any given key certain chords are more common than others. For example, in the key of **C,** the chords **C**, **F** and **G7** are usually present, and quite often the chords **Am, Dm** and **Em** occur. The reason for this is that each key has its own set of chords that are constructed from notes of its major scale. These chords are referred to as "scale tone" chords.

Consider the **C** major scale:

Note	C	D	E	F	G	A	B	C
Scale Number	1	2	3	4	5	6	7	8

Basic chords are constructed by combining notes which are a third apart. For example, consider the formula for a major chord.

Using the **C** major scale written above, scale tone chords can be constructed by placing two intervals of a 3rd above each note. This is illustrated in the following table.

5	G	A	B	C	D	E	F	G
3	E	F	G	A	B	C	D	E
C Scale: 1	C	D	E	F	G	A	B	C
Chord Constructed:	C	Dm	Em	F	G	Am	B°	C
Chord Numeral:	I	IIm	IIIm	IV	V	VIm	VII°	VIII

Third Interval
Third Interval

Notice that the chords are named according to their root note. However, they are all **C** scale tone chords because they contain only notes of the **C** scale (i.e. no sharps or flats).

The method used for constructing scale tone chords in the key of C may be applied to any major scale. The result will always produce the following scale tone chords:

Scale Note:	I	II	III	IV	V	VI	VII	VIII
Chord Constructed:	major	minor	minor	major	major	minor	dim	major

Thus in the key of **G** major, the scale tone chords will be:

G Am Bm C D Em F♯° G

and in the key of E♭ major, the scale tone chords will be:

E♭ Fm Gm A♭ B♭ Cm D° E♭

Summary of Scale Tone Chords

Scale Note:	I	II	III	IV	V	VI	VII	VIII
Chord Constructed:	major	minor	minor	major	major	minor	dim	major
C Scale	C	Dm	Em	F	G	Am	B°	C
G Scale	G	Am	Bm	C	D	Em	F♯°	G
D Scale	D	Em	F♯m	G	A	Bm	C♯°	D
A Scale	A	Bm	C♯m	D	E	F♯m	G♯°	A
E Scale	E	F♯m	G♯m	A	B	C♯m	D♯°	E
B Scale	B	C♯m	D♯m	E	F♯	G♯m	A♯°	B
F♯ Scale	F♯	G♯m	A♯m	B	C♯	D♯m	E♯°(F°)	F♯
F Scale	F	Gm	Am	B♭	C	Dm	E°	F
B♭ Scale	B♭	Cm	Dm	E♭	F	Gm	A°	B♭
E♭ Scale	E♭	Fm	Gm	A♭	B♭	Cm	D°	E♭
A♭ Scale	A♭	B♭m	Cm	D♭	E♭	Fm	G°	A♭
D♭ Scale	D♭	E♭m	Fm	G♭	A♭	B♭m	C°	D♭
G♭ Scale	G♭	A♭m(G♯m)	B♭m	C♭(B)	D♭	E♭m	F°	G♭

Scale Tone Chord Extensions

The scale tone chords studied so far involve the placement of two notes (separated by an interval of a third) above a root note. This method of building scale tone chords can be extended by adding another note of a third interval, illustrated in the following table:

7	B	C	D	E	F	G	A	B		Third Interval
5	G	A	B	C	D	E	F	G		Third Interval
3	E	F	G	A	B	C	D	E		Third Interval
C Scale: 1	C	D	E	F	G	A	B	C		Third Interval
Chord Constructed:	Cmaj7	Dm7	Em7	Fmaj7	G7	Am7	Bm7♭5*	Cmaj7		
Chord Numeral:	Imaj7	IIm7	IIIm7	IVmaj7	V7	VIm7	VIIm7♭5	Imaj7		

*Another name for a minor seven flat five chord is half-diminished, indicated thus ⌀.

From this example, the scale tone chords for any key will be:

I	II	III	IV	V	VI	VII	VIII
major7	m7	m7	maj7	7	m7	m7♭5 or (⌀7)	maj7

Summary of Scale Tone Extension Chords

I	II	III	IV	V	VI	VII	VIII
Major7	**Minor7**	**Minor7**	**Major7**	**7**	**Minor7**	**Minor7♭5**	**Major7**
Cmaj7	Dm7	Em7	Fmaj7	G7	Am7	Bm7♭5	Cmaj7
Gmaj7	Am7	Bm7	Cmaj7	D7	Em7	F#m7♭5	Gmaj7
Dmaj7	Em7	F#m7	Gmaj7	A7	Bm7	C#m7♭5	Dmaj7
Amaj7	Bm7	C#m7	Dmaj7	E7	F#m7	G#m7♭5	Amaj7
Emaj7	F#m7	G#m7	Amaj7	B7	C#m7	D#m7♭5	Emaj7
Bmaj7	C#m7	D#m7	Emaj7	F#7	G#m7	A#m7♭5	Bmaj7
F#maj7	G#m7	A#m7	Bmaj7	C#7	D#m7	E#(F)m7♭5	F#maj7
Fmaj7	Gm7	Am7	B♭maj7	C7	Dm7	Em7♭5	Fmaj7
B♭maj7	Cm7	Dm7	E♭maj7	F7	Gm7	Am7♭5	B♭maj7
E♭maj7	Fm7	Gm7	A♭maj7	B♭7	Cm7	Dm7♭5	E♭maj7
A♭maj7	B♭m7	Cm7	D♭maj7	E♭7	Fm7	Gm7♭5	A♭maj7
D♭maj7	E♭m7	Fm7	G♭maj7	A♭7	B♭m7	Cm7♭5	D♭maj7
G♭maj7	A♭m7	B♭m7	C♭(B) maj7	D♭7	E♭m7	Fm7♭5	G♭maj7